DEVELOPING LEARNING HABITS

Seven Steps to Successful Change

Book 2 of the **MAXIMISING BRAIN POTENTIAL** series

Dr. Celine Mullins

With Guest Author Dr. Richard Roche

·OAK·TREE·PRESS·

Published by Oak Tree Press, Cork, Ireland

www.oaktreepress.com / www.SuccessStore.com

ISBN: 978-1-78119-459-1 (Paperback)

ISBN: 978-1-78119-343-3 (ePub)

ISBN: 978-1-78119-344-0 (Kindle)

ISBN: 978-1-78119-345-7 (PDF)

Cover by Ian Johnston

Brain Images by Phillip Cullen

CONTENTS

FOREWORD

Some books are beautifully timed, others miss their moment by being too late to market or too far ahead. This book is the right book at the right moment. The idea of successful behaviour change is the *sine qua non* of learning and development. We have always known that; however, it has taken a global pandemic to create a sense of urgency about making learning and development more efficient and more effective. If that is your task, take this book with you on the journey.

Using a mixture of psychology, neuroscience and cognitive science research with learning and development insights, Celine Mullins (joined by Cognitive Neuroscientist Richard Roche), has created a simple, straight forward and eminently useful volume. It outlines seven fundamental steps to better learning and permanent habit change. These range from building clarity to understanding memory and making things memorable.

But what I liked most was the section on feeling awareness (HOW). What Celine clearly demonstrates is that successful behaviour change requires both psychological safety and a sense of meaningful engagement with the learning in question. Every person working in learning and development should, at the least, read this section to understand a fundamental part of how learning works in our brain.

This book is about 100 pages long, yet it is packed full of practical, insightful and evidence-based steps to create better learning that will change people's learning behaviour forever. There is nothing more important, right now, than trying to understand the learners you want to influence and the most efficient and effective ways of doing this.

This is a sharp, well-researched practical book that will resonate with everybody. I learned a lot reading it, and I am sure that you will too. If I have to pick just one sentence from the book that sums up why I think it is so useful it is this: "Engaging as much of the brain and body as we possibly can, will assist long-term change". That is an excellent mantra and something we should probably write on a piece of paper and tape it above our desk because science now shows us that learning and habit change is a full body experience. I highly recommend this book.

Nigel Paine, Change-Focused Leader: Leadership, Innovation, Learning & Technology

Leadership & Learning Consultant (**nigelpaine.com**) and Academic Director of Penn CLO Doctoral Program at the University of Pennsylvania. Professorship from Napier University in Edinburgh, Fellow of the CIPD, LPI, the RSA and a Masie Learning Fellow in the USA. Author of eight books, including *The Learning Challenge: Dealing with Technology, Innovation and Change in Learning and Development; Building Leadership Development Programmes: Zero-Cost to High-Investment Programmes that Work; Workplace Learning: How to Build a Culture of Continuous Employee Development* (all published by Kogan Page). Presenter of a monthly TV programme (Learning Now TV), and co-host of a weekly podcast (with Martin Couzins) called *From Scratch*.

A NOTE FROM THE AUTHOR

We are what we repeatedly do. Excellence, then, is not an act, but a habit.

Aristotle[1]

Are you making the most of your learning potential?

During my time working as a facilitator of learning and growth, I have had the opportunity to observe how we behave as individuals, teams and organisations. Cognitive science, psychology and neuroscience have taught us a lot about the 'how' and 'why' of our behaviour as humans. Only the smartest organisations and educational institutions have taken what is applicable from these schools of theory and research and have applied it to how we learn and change behaviours. And this is a work in progress for everyone involved.

If like me, and many others I know, you have read books, listened to podcasts, attended workshops and webinars, and thereafter made few changes in your behaviour, then welcome to the club. There are many reasons for not making the planned changes that might surprise you – and they are covered in this book. Time and time again, in recent years I see the difference that knowing this information makes to a person's commitment to change and to their own long-term behavioural change.

Depending on your own experience, reading this book will help you to see learning from new or different perspectives. Awareness of the concepts in this book will help you to open up to learning new things and enable you to maintain the elements that make long-term behavioural change possible.

How do I know this works?

With my clients over the years, I have learned by observing what is effective and what is not in creating change. People who have taken on this information have made long-term behavioural change, while those who have not often have not had the same success.

This book is the second in the MAXIMISING BRAIN POTENTIAL series. This series is as much as possible based on the most up-to-date scientific research combined with my experience of working in the area of change as to how our brain and body potential can be maximised for habit change, learning, productivity and health.

Please note, I am neither a neuroscientist, nor a cognitive scientist. I am a psychologist and coach. The focus for me in writing these books is to pull useful information together into digestible chunks. Therefore, at times, I will leave out granular details about the brain and details from research (including many articles and books I have read) that would get in the way of applying the findings in practical ways.

The other books in the series include OUR LEARNING BRAIN: How to Teach Your Brain to Learn New Habits and CHANGE BEGINS HERE: Building The Foundations For Learning & Habit Change. These books introduce additional concepts and also probe deeper into some of the topics discussed in this book.

Similar to the current wave of just-in-time learning, where learning is available on-demand, and can be accessed when the learner needs it, the MAXIMISING BRAIN POTENTIAL series of books is just-what-you-need-to-know-to-make learning-easier in adulthood.

I know this text will be useful for you, whether you want to make a change in your own life, or you are involved in helping others learn and make change.

If you would like more support applying this information in your organisation, we also provide workshops on these topics, and have an online course available. Contact **info@adaptastraining.com** for information.

Dr. Celine Mullins, Adaptas

4

ACKNOWLEDGEMENTS

Thank you to Diana Friedman for once again having so much patience and taking care in reading, editing, re-reading, and editing this book many times over the course of a few years! Having initially thought this book was ready to follow hot on the heels of Book 1: **Our Learning Brain** in 2018, Diana helped me to see the light!

Thank you to Nigel Paine for taking the time to read the 'almost ready' manuscript, and urging me to release the book into the world. Also, for his kind foreword and ongoing encouragement, support and friendship.

Thank you once again to Brian at Oak Tree Press for seeing the potential a number of years ago on receiving a version of the manuscript, and for patience with each 'near final draft' email!

Thank you to Janet Kane for patient checking of references and notes, for a keen eye on fonts, spellings, and grammar and much more. And for generally being an incredible addition to Adaptas and to my life.

Thank you to Alistair McBride and Erika Brodnock for input and for being trusted friends and colleagues.

Thank you to Siobhan Brennan, Owen Murray, Jamie Cole and Niall Watters for reading, suggesting edits, reporting back 'success' in using the information, and ongoing encouragement.

Thank you to Emma Smith, Regina O'Loughlin and Aoife McNamee for reading and for chunking the information down to assist in the build of the online course.

Thank you also to Annika McGivern for reading and providing me with feedback, and helping with the build of the online course.

Thank you to my brother David Mullins for sending Annika my way!

Thank you to Claire Comerford and Enda Hughes for pushing me out of my comfort zone and encouraging me to do more with my writing, beyond blogs etc.

Thank you to my family for understanding that weekends and evenings are the only time I can get time to work on my books.

Thank you to Dr. Richard Roche for once again being my second pair of eyes with the cognitive neuroscience and for adding his knowledge and passion for the subject to this book by way of contributing a section on the importance of memory for learning (**Step 4**).

And a final huge thank you to my clients, without whom these books would simply not exist. I share some examples of clients I have worked with but have changed some names and small details to protect their anonymity.

WHY READ THIS BOOK?

It will help you to **use your brain and body more effectively** when learning new skills by offering simple and practical tips.

It will support you in **breaking old habits and creating new ones**.

It will give you useful **insights into organisational learning and development-related topics** that you can easily put into context whether you are in a Learning & Development, Talent Management or Change Management position, or a manager and leader of people who needs to motivate your staff to learn and perform.

It will offer you **useful, practical recommendations based on our experience at Adaptas** in combination with findings from decades of research in cognitive science, neuropsychology and more.

INTRODUCTION

Have you ever attended a learning event, in person or online, where you have taken lots of written notes and made many mental notes? Then soon after you realise you have forgotten most of the advice, tools and techniques?

We've all been there. Many of us have tried to implement the information, tips, and techniques provided by the trainers, speakers or facilitators. Indeed, over recent years, organisations have invested significantly in learning and development. But for some reason, much of the learning doesn't stick.

Why is that?

When we were children, our brains were like sponges, soaking up new learning quite easily. But as adults a lot more effort is required to embed new learning and change old habits. We have to overcome the old habits, assumptions, and beliefs. When we learn something new, a signal travels along a nerve. It reaches a gap (synapse) and can go one of many ways. Will it go the old route or one of the many new routes it could take? In order to create new pathways that last, we need to use the same path again and again. As we do, the brain rebuilds itself to make the signal stronger and therefore easier to embed. In a nutshell, the consolidation of new neural pathways takes much longer than the duration of our initial motivation to make the change in the first place.

Take two people in management roles at the same organisation who attended a leadership development programme: Catherine and Jim. One of the modules was focused on communication topics such as communicating for impact, and improving performance appraisal and difficult conversations.

Jim was keen to try a few of the tips that he had taken from this module. He had experienced, during the roleplay sessions, the differences that could be made by asking more open questions and listening more and thus creating real two-way communication. On returning to work, he attempted to have a difficult conversation that he'd been putting off for ages. The new approach didn't work well for him with his colleague. This was partly because Jim tried to change his entire approach. His colleague recognised Jim wasn't being authentically 'Jim'. Both parties felt uncomfortable. After this, Jim stopped attempting to implement or practice any elements of the new approach he had learned on the course for fear of messing up again. He reverted to what he had always done and later told me it was 'too hard to teach an old dog new tricks'.

Catherine was also keen to try out some of the tips from this module. Communication was something she knew she needed to work on. She believed she wasn't being assertive enough and that some of her team were taking advantage of this. She was very clear at the outset of the programme that this was something she wanted and needed to work on. On returning to work, she shared with some trusted colleagues the changes she wished to make and asked some of them to hold her accountable to these changes. She scheduled daily learning actions to change and improve her communication, focusing on changing one little thing at a time when she had conversations with colleagues. She tried a few things differently early on and made some quick wins. She focused on improving one element of communication at a time so that over time the changes would compound. She learnt from the outcomes and took all feedback graciously from her colleagues. She stuck with the process and ultimately made many improvements that lasted. Within six months her efforts were recognised with a promotion.

What was it that enabled Catherine's development and success compared to Jim's?

Catherine approached her learning and the application of her learning consciously. She made everything as tangible as she could so that she could take action, get feedback on that action, and repeat quickly. She didn't leave her learning and habit change to chance. If she noticed she wasn't taking action, she re-visited the elements that might be stopping her. And she did everything she could to involve others in the process.

Over the years, my experiences with Catherine and countless other people regarding how they make and successfully embed their learning – combined with evidence from cognitive science, neuroscience and psychology – have taught me that:

> Approaching habit change and learning with conscious choice and awareness yields results quicker. We've got to use our brain and bodies effectively rather than letting them use us!

There are seven main steps that can be revisited over and over in the process of change and learning in order to embed long-term change. Learning and habit change is a process, not a once-off event. Taking the information in and hoping it will stick is not enough.

If we want to embed the learning, the environment and culture we put in place needs to enable the process.

These three concepts are threaded throughout the book, which is divided in to two parts. **Part I** addresses how building conscious choice and awareness yields results. **Part II** focuses on how we build long-term behavioural change consciously *via* the seven steps and also how we can use these seven steps to create a personal culture of learning and a culture of learning for others. Let me take you through these three main concepts very briefly now before we move on.

Building Conscious Choice and Awareness Yields Results

We cannot change what we are not aware of, and once we are aware, we cannot help but change.

Sheryl Sandberg[2]

These days, when I start working with a new person, group or team, I can usually tell very quickly who among them will make changes in how they operate. I have seen numerous people welcome the concepts discussed in this book and also in Book 1 of this series: **Our Learning Brain**. I have observed people make conscious choices, and take deliberate action towards the change they want to make. They follow the steps and the exercises set to build awareness of their actions, rather than leave it to chance.

Part I will explain why approaching habit change and learning with conscious choice and awareness yields results quicker than simply placing all your hope in the desire to make change and letting your automatic nature take its course.

Long-Term Behavioural Change: A Seven Step Process

> *Learning is a process, not an event.*
>
> Elliott Masie[3]

Too often learning is treated as an event, whether it is a topic delivered by a speaker, facilitator or an online modular course. New information often takes months to embed and become behavioural change. It must be a process, not an event. Too often though, people are not given, or do not find the tools to help this information embed.

Over the years, I have explored what processes can help people make their behavioural change 'stick' long-term. Through this work, I have developed a sequence of seven steps that can counteract old patterning and help develop learning and habit change. As I tested out these steps, I realised that they could be used when we are initially working out what we want to do differently. And once we have the ball rolling, we need to continue to use these steps until the change sticks.

If these seven steps are followed consecutively, simultaneously and continuously, they will help neural changes to take place in your brain, helping you to form new habits and enabling the learning to stick long-term. **Part II** will take you through the steps and the science behind these steps so that you can understand the 'what', 'why' and the 'how' of the change you want to make.

Learning Requires Creating A Culture of Learning

> *Continuous learning leads to continuous improvement. Commit yourself to advancing your knowledge, skills, and expertise. The business environment is quickly changing, and your understanding of the leading practices, thinking, and emerging tools will help you manage for better results. Be a lifelong student.*
>
> Pamela Gill Alabaster[4]

In some of the most progressive organisations globally, a learning culture has been successfully created. In these cultures, it is recognised that every opportunity should be given to learning and mastering new skills and to encouraging a growth mindset. However, in many organisations, learning is often still isolated from the work itself. With the greatest intentions, people can't always find time outside of role responsibilities to prioritise focus toward this, even though it's as important as the work itself. Research recently conducted at LinkedIn[5] found that employees who spend time at work learning are 47% less likely to be stressed, 39% more likely to feel productive and successful, 23% more ready to take on additional responsibilities, and 21% more likely to feel confident and happy. Creating this culture of learning requires role-modelling and encouragement of learning from top-down in the organisation, as well as openness to failure and feedback at all levels. Creating an organisation-wide culture of learning is beyond the scope of this book. For this, I highly recommend reading Nigel Paine's book *Workplace Learning: How to Build a Culture of Continuous Employee Development.*

Throughout **Part II** of this book, however, there is a script of questions that you can use in your process of learning something new and in changing habits. This will help you to create a personal culture of learning. And if you are managing others, I invite you to use these topics and questions with your colleagues to help them to prioritise learning and to embed their learning and habit change over time. Thus, you will create a culture of learning within your own team.

PART I: BUILDING CONSCIOUS CHOICE AND AWARENESS YIELDS RESULTS

> *... we must make automatic and habitual, as early as possible, as many useful actions as we can ... The more details of our daily life we can hand over to the effortless custody of automatism, the higher mental powers of mind will be set free for their own proper work.*
>
> William James[6]

I have observed people make conscious choices and take deliberate action towards the change they want to make. They follow the steps and the exercises set to build awareness of their actions, rather than leave it to chance. I have seen them make very real change in their lives. I speak with these people many months or sometimes years after having worked with them on the changes they wanted to make. I hear of all the new habits that they have maintained, and the differences those new habits have made to their working lives. Many have impacted their lives outside of work also. They flip the switch to change how they are approaching and doing things and this switch remains flipped long-term.

I also meet others who never fully rise to the challenge. Some of them stop short because the change requires them to move too far out of their comfort zone. Some of them attempt to change their actions but they don't do the inner work. Doing the inner work enables people to overcome the beliefs and stories they hold about themselves and that are often keeping them stuck doing things the way they have always done them. Some people find every reason and explanation they can to argue why the change is not necessary, useful, or a good idea for them. And this is even though they tell me they want to make change or learn something new.

If you are reading this book, my guess is you're one of the proactive ones who is ready to recognise that you have more choice than you might think, that you are keen to build your awareness, and that you wish to take deliberate action to create positive change!

The three main ideas to consider in building conscious choice and awareness are:

The unconscious mind.

The chemicals of learning.

Self-protection.

The Unconscious Mind

An enormous portion of cognitive activity is non-conscious, figuratively speaking, it could be 99 percent; we probably will never know precisely how much is outside awareness.

Emanuel Donchin[7]

When left to its own devices, the brain goes into automatic mode with everything. Studies indicate that nearly 50% of behaviours are repeated in the same circumstances almost every day.[8]

Much of how we operate is automatic: our behaviour, habits and patterns often run unconsciously without us having any awareness of them.

There is no real way to measure the processing capacity of the 'unconscious mind', partly because there is no definition for what it is, other than the 'mind' minus everything that is conscious. For example, it has been stated by many that the human eye sends approximately 10 million bits per second to the brain for processing, yet the conscious mind seems to be able to process only 50-60 bits per second.[9]

The vast majority of processing of the information is accomplished outside conscious notice. Even such a 'simple' activity as walking is best done without interference from consciousness, which does not have enough information processing capability to keep up with the demands of this task. If we were aware of everything going on inside our bodies and in the environment around us, we would implode.

Behavioural economists, cognitive psychologists, neuroscientists to name a few, have argued that a good deal of our mental life happens without our knowing much about it. The unconscious mind controls much of our behaviour. It has proved a source of considerable frustration because it defies objective description, and is extremely difficult to objectively test or measure.

It's fine to let our brain go into automatic pilot. But to overcome old ways of doing things, we need to understand our mental life beyond the actions, thoughts and feelings that we are conscious of in the moment. It takes conscious effort to make the unconscious become conscious, so that we can work with it. We have to pay attention to what we are doing automatically, if we are going to create change.

> *Sitting on your shoulders is the most complicated object in the known universe.*
>
> Michio Kaku[10]

If we understand that the unconscious mind is running us, we are more equipped to overcome it and more likely to make the changes we want to make for the long-term. If we want to do things differently, we must make the unconscious conscious. And then over time, we literally need to train circuits in the brain to carry out new actions until the new actions become the new 'automatic'.

Jim (from the leadership programme) is a great example of NOT making the unconscious conscious. He made it too easy for himself to let the automatic beliefs and habits win out. To successfully change his behaviour, Jim needed to break it all down, just like Catherine did. Jim would have been more likely to create long-lasting change by:

1. Identifying his automatic behaviours.
2. Learning new skills and behaviours
3. Practicing the new behaviours until they became automatic (replacing the old behaviours).

Jim completed the second but didn't completely fulfil the first or the third point.

> *For habits, what we tend to do in the present is what we have tended to do in the past whether we intend to do so or not.*
>
> Galla & Duckworth (2015)[11]

A useful model for thinking about our unconscious behaviours is the two-system model, originally proposed by psychologists Keith Stanovich and Richard West[12] and developed by Daniel Kahneman and Amos Tversky. Daniel Kahneman, a Nobel Prize winner and the intellectual godfather of behavioural economics, summarised a lifetime of research by himself, Tversky and colleagues in his book *Thinking Fast and Slow* (2011).[13]

In this model, the two systems that drive the way we think and behave are:

System 1: Automatic, fast, intuitive, and emotional.

System 2: Effortful, slow, deliberate, logical.

It is System 1 that reaches for the pastry when we are trying to eat healthily. It is System 1 that swerves the car to avoid the person who just crossed the road without looking left and right. It is System 1 that won out in Jim when he continued to micro-manage his colleagues, even though he had learned on the leadership programme that what he viewed as being 'helpful' and 'getting the job done', others saw as 'controlling'. System 1 is everything we do unconsciously.

System 2 involves bringing more conscious or effortful awareness to our thinking and behaviour. It is System 2 that swings into action when we have just picked up the rental car and have to drive on the other side of the road in a new country. It is System 2 that starts to work when you have to fill in a complicated document for your taxes, or a job application for a role you have not held previously. Or during a performance review conversation, when Catherine's colleague Ann reacted emotionally to the feedback being received, Catherine had to engage System 2 which helped her keep her cool to let Ann have her say. It was System 2 that listened patiently and focused on asking open questions to understand Ann's frustration, rather than attempting to explain away the reasons, and hence run the risk of frustrating Ann even more (which is what System 1 will do).

System 1 evolved in response to the need to obtain quick answers. Over here is a tiger: danger! Over there are berries: delicious! Those who needed to think slowly and carefully to arrive at these conclusions did not survive to become our ancestors.

System 1's operations involve no sense of intentional control, but it's the "secret author of many of the choices and judgements you make" (Kahneman, 2011). System 1 takes visible evidence as the only source of knowledge, and ignores hidden evidence. It doesn't mind working all the time, because its work is not that hard.

System 2's operations require attention. System 2 takes over, rather unwillingly, when things get difficult or challenging. We all like to think we are mostly System 2. Most of us believe that we are rational and logical beings. Kahneman compares System 2 to "a supporting character who believes herself to be the lead actor and often has little idea of what's going on", because System 1 responds quickly and automatically without getting System 2 to engage. So, in fact, we are largely System 1 most of the time.

System 2 is slothful, and tires easily (a process called 'ego depletion') – so it usually accepts what System 1 tells it. It's often right to do so, because System 1 is for the most part pretty good at what it does. It's highly sensitive to subtle environmental cues, signs of danger, and so on. As stated above, it kept our remote ancestors alive and serves many functions to this day.

When you engage in intense System 2 thinking, Kahneman says, something happens to your body. It requires so much effort that it takes over the whole body, so it goes to work only reluctantly. Your pupils dilate. Your heart rate increases. Your blood glucose level drops. You may become irritable if someone or something interrupts your focus. You become partially deaf and partially blind to stimuli that ordinarily command your attention.

System 2 requires a lot of energy to run. This means that lack of sleep and insufficient nutrition or hydration can impact its ability to engage effectively. We could be hungry or tired, and somebody gives us news or feedback we weren't expecting or ready for. Because System 2 requires so much energy, instead of being balanced and flexible, we may react emotionally and we lose our ability to flex to the person or situation.

It is necessary to apply System 2 thinking if we are serious about coming to sensible answers to most questions and to making changes in how we approach life and work.

Consider what Jim and Catherine learned at that leadership programme on the communication module. We've all been there, at a talk or workshop, reading a book or watching an online video. Afterwards, we try to apply it in real time even though it doesn't feel like second nature. It is System 1 that reverts to the old way of doing things. It is System 2 that makes a concerted effort to slow down and try something a different way. Jim engaged System 2 the first time he attempted to have a conversation a different way. But when it felt uncomfortable, and possibly like too much effort he reverted to System 1. Whereas Catherine pushed through and continued to keep System 2 engaged. Of course, neither Jim or Catherine were conscious that System 1 or 2 were taking over at the time. The only difference was that Catherine understood that she needed to remain deliberate in her actions in order to change the old habits, and that consolidation of her new learning would take time and conscious effort.

Most of the time System 1 runs automatically and System 2 is in a comfortable low-effort mode in the background. When the two agree, impressions get turned into beliefs. When System 1 runs into trouble, it asks for processing help from System 2.

System 1 is a very good system that works very well most of the time but it has systematic errors (works quickly, is emotional, has biases) and much of Kahneman's research is focused on identifying these.

The decisions we make and the actions we take are running instinctively and automatically. Therefore, when it comes to creating new habits and behaviours, we need to use this knowledge to effectively create change or embed the new learning. If we want to make change, we have to work harder than most of us would like. It takes effort, a lot of conscious awareness and moment-to-moment choice, to implement change that our body and brain will accept long-term!

The Chemicals of Learning

The adult male human brain, weighing on average 1.5 kg, contains on average 86 billion neurons.

Azevedo et al. (2009)[14]

Our thoughts, learning and behaviour are the result of some pretty complex chemistry. I don't want to overcomplicate learning and habit change, as it is challenging enough to create change in ourselves. However, I want us to take a light touch consideration of just some of the hormones and neurotransmitters involved in these processes. When we can put a name on the chemical we are looking to increase or decrease, it can help us make better decisions on where our focus goes and how we respond to events.

Hormones and neurotransmitters act as chemical messengers in the body. When we change behaviour, we release hormones and neurotransmitters. Depending on what we are experiencing and focusing on, the levels of these will increase or decrease. The chemicals involved include:

Acetylcholine: Acetylcholine, is the principal neurotransmitter involved in thought, learning, attention and memory.[15] We know that it is involved in memory because damage to the acetylcholine-producing areas of the brain have been linked with the memory deficits associated with Alzheimer's disease. And when we are learning something new, acetylcholine helps embed the learning. Acetylcholine is associated with REM sleep, and therefore we need to get plenty of sleep or at least regular naps to cement the new learning.

Glutamate: Glutamate is important for learning and memory. It regulates brain development and plays a major role in synaptic plasticity (the ability of synapses to strengthen or weaken over time, in response to increases or decreases in their activity). It influences the brain's ability to continuously adapt throughout a person's life so as to preserve health and cognitive function.

Serotonin: Serotonin is thought to be a contributor to feelings of well-being and happiness. Some research has linked it with memory and neuroplasticity.[16] More recent research[17] has shown that serotonin appears to contribute to the speed at which we learn new information.

Endorphin: Endorphins produce feelings of well-being or even euphoria and are released in the brain during exercise, excitement, pain, and sexual activity. Endorphins promote learning,[18] possibly because they impact reward centres of the brain (see dopamine below) – you will most likely remember the feeling you get from when you are doing or have completed exercise that gets your heart pumping faster, or when you listen to music you love. Many argue that learning leads to happiness and happiness leads to learning. There is no doubt that we tend to learn better and feel motivated to keep up good habits when are in a feel-good frame of mind.

Epinephrine: Previously known as adrenaline, epinephrine is a hormone produced in high stress or exciting situations. It is often referred to as the 'fight or flight' transmitter and it's what many of us refer to as the 'adrenaline rush'. This is important for us at adults when attempting to learn something new. Epinephrine

19

stimulates increased heart rate, contracts blood vessels, and dilates airways, to increase blood flow to the muscles and oxygen to the lungs. This leads to a physical boost and heightened awareness. When the body is flooded with epinephrine, the brain is engaged, focused, and able to handle cognitive tasks more quickly. Researchers have compared the boost in alertness to drinking coffee. Epinephrine is important to get us engaged and focused and therefore help with learning new information and creating habit change. Emotionally significant experiences, where the need to change feels urgently important tend to be well remembered. Therefore, when we are learning new material as adults, it's important to consider how we can make it meaningful and engage feelings and senses throughout our body. Of course, there is a certain point at which too much of a good thing in keeping us focused becomes stressful. There is a fine line with regard to the balance of focus and stress. In **Part II**, the steps to change will help you consider that balance for yourself.

Dopamine: Dopamine is associated with anticipation and reward, which of course is important in learning. It is also associated with doing something we enjoy and when we feel motivated.[19] Dopamine consolidates new circuits and causes addiction.[20] Addiction, like any other behavioural phenomenon, involves a plastic change in the brain.[21] The feelings of satisfaction caused by dopamine can become desired, and to satisfy them the person will repeat behaviours that lead to release of dopamine.

Many people, try as they may, find it extremely difficult not to continuously check for 'likes' or comments once they have posted an update. And we see it with certain recreational drugs and gambling. The addict feels like they can't live without their next 'hit'. They need the next hit to get the rush of dopamine (pleasure). Interestingly, more recent research finds that it is anticipation of the event, rather than the event itself that creates the surge in dopamine.[22]

Robert Sapolsky discusses this phenomenon in his book *Monkeyluv*.[23]

A neuroscientist named Wolfram Schultz, then at the University of Fribourg in Switzerland, did some critical studies. He would train a monkey in a task. A light comes on, signalling the beginning of the reward period. This means that if the monkey presses a lever X number of times, after a few seconds' delay it will receive a bit of some desirable food. Thus one would predict that the dopaminergic pathway becomes activated after that food reward. But no. When does activity peak? Right after the light comes on, before the monkey performs its task. In this context, the pleasurable dopamine isn't about reward. It's about the anticipation of reward. It's about mastery and expectation and confidence. It's "I know what that light means. I know the rules: if I press the lever, then I'm going to get some food. I'm all over this. This is going to be great." The pleasure is in the anticipation of a reward; from the standpoint of dopamine, the reward is an afterthought.

Our brains work a lot like monkey brains. Our brains react to anticipation and dopamine in the same way.

Developing Learning Habits

We've all had the experience in adulthood of attempting to learn something new or changing a habit and falling short of making it stick long-term. Sadly, learning and change takes a lot more effort than when we were children, for a whole host of reasons including our brain and body's resistance to change and our engrained unconscious habits (neural pathways). The consolidation of new neural pathways takes longer than the motivation to change or learn lasts. Whether we are looking to create new habits or interested in encouraging others to learn, change takes planning and discipline in order to build repetition. When we decide to do something a new way, our motivation only lasts so long. A lot of us have a negative association the word 'discipline'.

However, if we consider the biological processes that involve reward pathways in the brain, we can understand how to take advantage of this process to help us develop and continue the new behaviours that we want to follow.

21

The reward circuits provide rushes of positive feeling and feel-good chemicals – endorphins – to 'reward' whatever it is we are doing. Therefore, we need to consider what can be put in place that motivates us and then keeps us accountable to repeating new behaviours and obtaining a positive feeling over and over again, after the motivation to take the action has waned. We need to find a way to want to repeat until the new behaviour is consolidated. Consolidation – influenced, for example, by levels of glutamate – takes time and repetition and much conscious choice to keep us on the track towards long-term success with the change.

Let's consider Catherine. She was very smart and others recognised her potential. But she did not fully recognise it in herself yet. Her confidence was low when she entered the programme, and there was a high chance she would fall off the wagon of learning and change when it came to being more assertive and impactful as a communicator and manager. So, at the outset, she got really clear on why she wanted to make changes. She worked daily on overcoming the limiting beliefs, that made her feel negative or unworthy of a promotion (serotonin). And she built in encouraging and constructive feedback from colleagues to make sure she stuck with her plan to create change: strengthening her focus and the synapses (acetylcholine & glutamate). This helped her to stay on track because it increased the production of dopamine (focus and pleasure), serotonin (feel good) and oxytocin (feel good and connection with others) and acetylcholine (attention, memory and consolidation).

At this point, I invite you to consider any behavioural change you have attempted and succeeded to embed long-term in recent years. On reflection, what little things did you do to create consolidation of the change that you desired? Little things go a long way over time to embed learning and to create change.

Self-Protection & Change

As we know, Jim took some tips from the communication module, went back to work, and had a difficult conversation with someone on his team that he'd been putting off for ages. Jim tried to structure his conversation differently to the way he would usually do it, and he tried to 'speak' and 'explain' less than he usually would. The plan was to have his colleague take 'ownership' of the issue and suggest what he might do or need to change, rather than Jim spoon-feeding him with all the solutions.

The conversation didn't go to plan for Jim. He felt uncomfortable because he wasn't used to asking questions and just 'shutting up'. After that, he never tried out the communication techniques again, even though he experienced them working at the programme he attended during roleplay conversations, and he knew that his colleagues from the programme were reporting great success with the techniques and approach. Why didn't Jim give it another go?

The answer is that we have an inbuilt biological drive for self-protection, and the brain is focused on energy saving. This often hinders our learning and habit change. In the first book of this series, **Our Learning Brain**, in Chapter 2, I discuss this in detail. Here is a quick summary and a few things to think about. We can also consider Jim in light of this information.

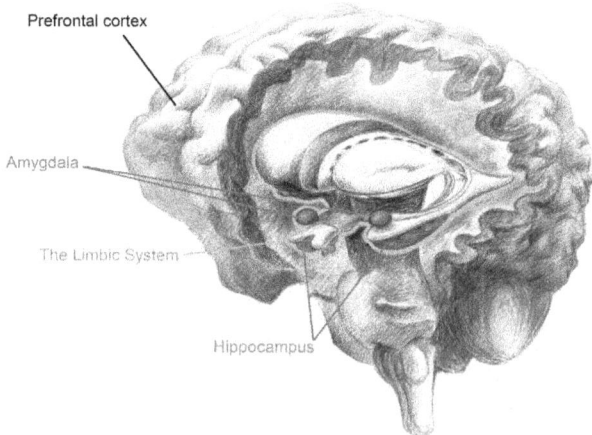

Figure 1: The Prefrontal Cortex and the Limbic System,
including Amygdala and Hippocampus

Even when you want to make a change in how you operate, the brain has a huge urge to protect you. When you start to think about doing something a different way and you start to believe that this change is possible, your Left Prefrontal Cortex (LPFC) – the area of the brain above your left eye – will focus on getting that done. However, very quickly, for many of us, fear of failure or fear of the unknown can activate the emotional systems of the brain, including an area known as the amygdala.

The amygdala is a small almond-shaped structure that sits directly in the limbic system in each hemisphere, in front of the hippocampus. The amygdalae (plural) have a particular role in how we experience emotions and memories, with the predominant role being the detection of emotionally-arousing cues (both aversive and pleasant) and subsequent activation of our motivational circuitry.

When you start to do something a different way, the brain and body work out very quickly that you are disturbing homeostasis. Blood flows towards these older areas of the brain, and the amygdala can set off a whole lot of sequences that put your brain and body into fight, flight or freeze. This can make it challenging for the LPFC to keep focused on achieving the outcome, you want because the blood is flowing away from it towards the more primitive parts of the brain. You could say your brain is rebelling against what you want to do. This happens because the brain is focused on working as efficiently as it can to keep you safe. And the amygdala can experience a change in habit as dangerous.

You will probably not even feel conscious of a need to fight or flee. All that will happen is that the stories, limiting beliefs and excuses will start rolling in. For example:

"My manager doesn't listen to me and I still do a good job. Why should I learn to be a better listener? It won't make me a better manager."

"I'll get one of my colleagues to make the presentation next week. I might let the team down if I present."

"I'm not good enough."

"I'll have deep fried calamari and fries for lunch one more time today, because I won't get time for dinner later. I'll start on the salads tomorrow!".

In the case of our friend Jim, the stories that crept in were *"I'm making a fool of myself"* and *"I'm too old to change how I manage people. It's all worked so far for me, why should I change things?".*

24

To create change and move past procrastination, we have to become conscious of our stories and limiting beliefs. Once conscious of them we have to push through the fight, flight or freeze to the other side.

It's useful to consider also the theory of 'loss aversion' (Kahneman & Tversky, 1979).[24] This refers to our strong preference for minimising losses over acquiring gains. Over many decades and through numerous studies, Kahneman & Tversky continually found that people prefer avoiding losses to acquiring equivalent gains. For example, in one of their studies, which they repeated and other researchers have since duplicated, they found that most people believe it's better to not lose €5 than to find €5. We feel almost twice the emotion over a loss as opposed to a gain.

Changing how we do things in life and work can be challenging because it feels like loss. The loss of the familiar is immediate and significant. For example, if I no longer have the couch and TV to look forward to every evening because I have decided I will attend a gym, it can feel like loss of comfort. Additionally, the gain is distant in both time and in relation to myself and the so-called gain is really more abstract than real, meaning that the incentive to pursue the change is not optimum. It is going to take weeks and maybe months before I notice the impact of going to the gym. Indeed, I may even feel worse for a few weeks because my body is not used to this level of energy consumption or the muscle pain!

To make real lasting change, you will have to manage your amygdala, which means managing your stories, excuses and emotions. As alluded to above, with the fear of failure, the difficult part is that you may not even be conscious of that fear. Our brain's unconscious operating system runs automatically and focuses on retaining energy and protecting us from any harm or discomfort.

When our brain tells us that 'change' is a harmful or a loss-inducing experience, we almost have to be ahead of it, to be able to fool it, if we are going to make a change. There are lots of ways to manage this. I discuss some of these in Book 1, **Our Learning Brain**, and more throughout this book.

Managing Change & Self-Protection in Organisations

If you are working as part of an organisation, be that a business, local community, educational or other, it is important to consider self-protection and loss. It doesn't matter if you are an individual attempting to learn a new skill or are part of a business or team being asked to increase or reduce a behaviour that, for example, will save a business money in the long-term or change the culture. Doing things a different way can often be associated with loss.

If you have ever been involved in making a change in any organisation, you will know that there are all sorts of change models that can be followed. All of these models refer in some way to engaging people in the solution or plan as early as possible towards co-creation and buy-in. Why?

In any organisational environment, where more than one person is involved there is the propensity for people to be unclear of their roles, or unclear of where the organisation is headed, or misunderstand why certain changes are taking place. Often the change is not a success. Or there are casualties along the way, such as disengagement, problems with retention of good staff or industrial disputes. If people are not completely clear on the benefits to them personally of the change, or do not feel safe with the actions being taken by their line managers and other decision-makers, many of the creative, innovative areas of the brain become deactivated.[25]

If we perceive the change as negative or we feel fearful (for example, "What if this change leads to my job becoming obsolete?"), our body will overproduce adrenaline and increase cortisol – the hormones associated with stress. These hormones will shut down our motivation by igniting the older fear circuits of the brain.

The role of the leader and manager is becoming more and more recognised as extremely important in embedding learning and change. Change is a process and overcoming fear is ongoing. The adult brain wants things to remain the way things have always been and the way we know things already work – even if that is not the best way.

To help people make change, it can be really useful to be supported by others in thinking differently for ourselves. This is a continuous process requiring a growth mindset and a culture that welcomes making mistakes, and giving and receiving feedback. It does not happen overnight. Even in organisations that change quickly, and where feedback is a mainstay of the culture, it is important to recognise that at least the majority of us have an inbuilt biological drive for self-protection. And, I've not yet in my years of working with people met one person who did not have at least one limiting belief.

This is the case even in the most innovative, fast-paced organisations and at all levels of the organisation. Many people just hide these beliefs very well from others. And they show up as other types of ineffective or off-putting behaviours.

In concluding **Part 1**, I hope you already have lots to think about. For many of us, successful adult learning and long-term habit change benefits greatly from being conscious of how the brain works. If we bring conscious awareness to our day-to-day thoughts and actions, we can make better choices in how we and others approach doing things differently.

In **Part II**, we'll build on what you now know and discuss the seven steps that can help you develop learning habits and create successful change.

> *Acknowledging the unproductive thoughts and ineffective behaviour that you've tried to ignore can be uncomfortable. But, stepping out of your comfort zone and choosing to proactively address bad habits will skyrocket your ability to create long-lasting change.*
>
> Amy Morin[26]

PART II: Seven Steps to Change and Creating A Culture of Learning

Human brains continuously undergo structural reorganization and functional changes in response to stimulations or training.

Cai et al. (2014)[27]

Change is sometimes a personal choice and other times caused by something external to us. External examples might include the organisation we are working with needing to take a different direction based on a new strategy. Or we've been asked to interview for a new role, which will involve more responsibility. Or the global pandemic we've recently witnessed which forced changes on the majority of us. Sometimes change comes from inside us: I decide I want to move to a different country and therefore need to learn a new language. Or I decide I want to get fitter. Or I go through a break-up and realise it's a similar issue that caused the previous break-up, and it's time to do a bit of personal development.

When initially we realise that it's time to do something differently, we go about change in our own habitual ways. Some of us experience fear and loss, even when the decision has come from inside ourselves. Sometimes our attempts to learn and change works for us and sometimes it doesn't. In my experience, change is not always easy. It's not enough to make the decision to do something in a different way. We are run by our habits, our values, and our beliefs.

This section explores the Seven Steps to Learning and Habit Change:

STEP 1: CLARITY: WHAT?

STEP 2: CURIOSITY: WHY?

STEP 3: FEELING AWARENESS: HOW?

STEP 4: MEMORY: WHEN & WHERE?

STEP 5: DEDICATION: HOW MANY?

STEP 6: ENVIRONMENT: WHO?

STEP 7: OBSTACLES: WHICH?

The purpose of these steps is to help us counteract old patterning and help make learning and habit change consolidation clearer and simpler. These steps can be considered when initially working out what specifically we want or need to do differently. Once we have the ball rolling on this, we can use these steps simultaneously and continuously. We might reach step 4, for example, and realise that it is helpful to return to Step 2 to re-consider it in light of Step 4.

I use open questions (WHAT?, WHY? etc) with each step, not to confuse, but to act as triggers. These triggers are easy to remember and can help keep us in a questioning, curious and growth mindset around the change we want to make.

Throughout **Part II**, and immediately after each step is explained, you will be prompted by extra questions that will help you work through the steps proactively.

Therefore, I advise that you prepare to read **Part II** while allowing yourself the time to reflect on your answers. Keep coming back to the questions posed as you attempt to change a habit or embed a new skill. There are certain steps that might feel more important to return to as you progress. You will be the best judge of that. Once you are on the road to embedding a change, you might wish to return to this text to approach the next change.

In my experience and the experience of countless others, if you stick to these steps you will have a much better chance of making the change, than leaving it to chance.

Note: If you prefer to print out a version of the worksheets with the questions for all steps, rather than write in this book, please see **www.adaptastraining.com/books**.

STEP 1: CLARITY: WHAT?

If your habits don't line up with your dream, then you need to either change your habits or change your dream.

John Maxwell[28]

When we consider the WHAT, there are three main ways of enriching clarity and focus towards the WHAT of real and lasting change:

> **Firstly**, getting as tangible as you can on WHAT it is that you want to do differently, because approaching it with broad strokes will hamper consolidation.

> **Secondly**, getting clarity of your self-identity and how you see yourself as an individual is important. Because if your self-identity does not match with your WHAT, it will be a challenge to create the change.

> **Thirdly**, engaging your imagination in using your senses as well as the feelings in your body to visualise the WHAT and the outcomes of the WHAT, will strengthen the chance of success.

Let's take each of these one at a time.

WHAT do I want to do differently?

This is the simplest part of the WHAT, but it is often bypassed by people looking to learn and create change.

Ask yourself: "WHAT do I want to do more of, less of or differently?".

This may seem ridiculously obvious. If you can get clarity on the specifics of WHAT you want to do or achieve, you are more likely to succeed in making the change. However, there is more than meets the eye on the WHAT. Most of us don't get specific and tangible enough.

For example, "I want to be a better communicator" is not as useful as "I want to let my colleagues know they are being listened to.

Therefore, in team and 1-2-1 meetings I will stay quiet and listen to my colleagues' ideas and opinions rather than interrupting". The latter is more specific and tangible, and already gives us something to clearly aim for, that is also in a sense observable and measurable. "I will eat three portions of vegetables every day; one at lunchtime and two with dinner" is more specific and tangible and therefore more effective in creating the change than "I want to eat healthier". And "I will do a weights session every Tuesday and Thursday at 5pm, and a yoga class every Saturday morning", is more tangible and specific than "I want to get fit".

Do you need to get more specific and tangible right now on your own WHAT?

Self-Identity and WHAT?

Once you have identified the WHAT, consider your self-identity. How do you view yourself as an individual? Self-identity is a combination between your actual experiences with the world around you, but also how you interpret those experiences and how you fit them into the narrative of *"This is me!"* and *"This isn't me!".* For example, *"I'm the type of person who puts my health first",* or *"I'm the type of person who believes it is important to treat others with kindness",* or *"I'm the type of parent who puts my children's happiness before my own".*

Consider the manager who swoops in to save everyone – 'the hero' – as many of the managers and leaders I have worked with over the years see themselves, although not always consciously. If this is your self-identity: *"I am the hero, this is me, this is who I am",* then is staying quiet, listening to and <u>not interrupting</u> your colleagues' ideas and opinions going to happen? Especially if you think their ideas are really crazy or you've seen these things trialled previously and they did not work?

It is going to require some work on firstly recognising your <u>self-identity</u> of *"I am the hero, this is me"* and then checking in on whether the change you want to make will be helped or hindered by that self-identity.

Or take the person who decided as part of her fitness regime to do yoga every week, because so many people recommended it to her to build her flexibility, and strength. She was a married woman with three children. She had always preferred team sports at school and never saw herself as the type of person who would spend time on a mat breathing and stretching. Committing to making it to the yoga classes was a challenge. Her self-identities of "*I am a wife*", "*I am a mother of three*", "*I prefer team sports*", "*I don't spend my time sitting around*" got in the way of making it to the regular practice of yoga. She did attend a few yoga classes. However, when it came to choosing between getting a little lie-in or the kids all wanted to go to the park or suddenly her husband had a really important call to take, or TV programme to watch, it became less and less likely for her to insist that her yoga class come first in her list of priorities.

We all have our own self-identity. None of them are right or wrong or to be judged. They just are.

Jim, who initially attempted to change some of his behaviours after the communication module on the leadership programme, ultimately was "*the type of manager who told people what to do*". He was a transactional manager and leader. He valued order and structure. He took pride in himself by completing objectives on time. Hence, he was not "*the type of person who gave people a wide berth and the support to learn how to do things their own way*". It was 'his way or the highway'. When he attended the leadership programme, he was not sufficiently uncomfortable or under pressure in his role, or enthused about doing things differently in order to change his self-identity about who he was or how he did things. He believed it hadn't failed him to date, so why should he change?

What I didn't mention earlier is that sadly for Jim, six months after attending that programme, the company management and structure changed. Jim was demoted from his role as a manager, specifically because he was not managing younger people the way they want to be managed. This eventually caused issues with retention and a decision was made to place him in a non-management role. This happened to Jim ultimately because his WHAT and his self-identity were not aligned.

So, once you have decided on your WHAT, check in with your self-identity. Here are some examples of self-identity that might block you from creating real and long-term change:

> "*When it comes to listening to others' ideas at work, I'm the type of person who gets the job done one way or another*".

"When it comes to learning new things, I'm the type of person who is very interested initially, but then I get distracted".

"When it comes to getting to the gym, I'm the type of person who goes four times per week for a month and then gives up".

Listen out for other people saying these things about themselves. We often tell other people "I'm the type of person who ...". We give ourselves and each other clues all the time.

Now consider WHAT you are looking to do more of, less of, or differently and fill in your blanks:

"When it comes to _____ (your new tangible WHAT), I'm the type of person who _____.

For example, *"when it comes to doing my weights session every Tuesday and Thursday and yoga every Saturday, I'm the type of person who knows that fitness and strength gives me more energy to my life".*

Having written that down, and reading back over it now, how does it sit for you? Might you need to be more honest with yourself? If your WHAT and self-identity are not aligned, might you need to put some support in place to ensure your learning or habit change? Once you are clear on WHAT you want to do differently, and that it is aligned to your self-identity, then it is very useful and powerful to consider this WHAT in more detail using your imagination and using visualisation. This is discussed in the subsequent sections.

Imagination and WHAT?

> *Imagination is more important than knowledge. For while knowledge defines all we currently know and understand, imagination points to all we might yet discover and create.*
>
> Albert Einstein[29]

Something that I have always found intriguing and may or may not be news to you, is that you can grow your skills by imagining yourself practising a skill, without ACTUALLY physically practicing that skill.[30]

Imagined outcomes of achieving the WHAT are really important. It's been shown that the brain makes connections between things that happen in real-time and predictions of all possible outcomes. The neural wiring blends together what is currently happening with the imagined predictions. In this way, the brain weaves its own explanation, or interpretation, of reality and this can be used as the basis of new skills formation.

Fundamentally, belief in the outcome significantly raises the likelihood of that outcome or associated behaviour occurring, be that outcome / behaviour positive or negative. If we want to do something differently or implement a new learned skill, we can start creating the new neural pathways by imagining the details of WHAT it is we want to do.

Please note, however that we need to get as specific and tangible as we can about the obstacles that will get in our way and make a plan to overcome these obstacles. Positive thinking or visualisation are not enough, and in fact may have the inverse affect with regard to us getting what we want.[31] The story is not complete without identifying the obstacles and creating a plan to overcome them. That's why you will learn about obstacles and how to overcome them later in these steps.

Visualisation of WHAT?

Visualisation is a technique that is useful in helping you with your WHAT. Athletes have known for years that visualisation techniques (otherwise known as mental practice or mental imagery) improve performance, motivation and focus. Many athletes also use visualisation to manage and reduce anxiety.

WHAT is Visualisation?

Visualisation is a cognitive tool accessing imagination to realise all aspects of an object, action or outcome. Visualisation involves creating a picture in your mind of WHAT you want to happen in reality. It can also be a 'stepping into' the feeling you would feel both during the unfolding of the 'WHAT' and at its culmination. While imagining a scenario, imagine as much detail as you can. Imagine the way it feels to perform in the desired way, including using all your senses and the feelings in your body associated with doing it. This mental and physical rehearsal helps our minds and bodies to become trained to actually perform the skill imagined.

Many studies have found this form of practice to be nearly as effective as physical practice for skills from types of shots taken in basketball and golf, to movement accuracy and velocity in pianists, to technical skills in novice surgeons.

For example, Pascual-Leone et al.[32] conducted a transcranial magnetic stimulation study, a technique to measure the activity and function of specific brain circuits, which showed that imagined practice (in this case of a piano sequence) led to comparable expansion of the cortical premotor areas responsible for controlling the fingers as actual physical practice.

So, you don't even have to actually move a finger to get the neurons communicating and the neural pathways forming and consolidating!

Using visualisation has now filtered from athletic endeavours into the business and the corporate world. Many highly successful people attribute their achievements to integrating this kind of neural influence with appropriate action.

Research has shown that self-efficacy is significantly higher and communication skills improved in supervisors when mental practice is used in combination with goal setting as a post-training intervention.[33]

Belief in the outcome significantly raises the likelihood of that outcome or behaviour associated occurring. However, the feeling throughout the process has to be as much as possible conducive to WHAT you desire. Otherwise it can hinder the likelihood of achieving the desired outcome. We will talk about this a little more later, but for now consider that you are going to be best served by focusing on WHAT you do want, rather than WHAT you don't want! This is important also to consider in creating and maintaining motivation, as we will discover later. If you are attempting to change how you do something or learning a new skill to move away from something – for example, "I don't want to fail my exams" – you are more likely to achieve the goal by visualising yourself opening up the email with your results where you pass with 'flying colours' rather than imagining the opposite. The focus on WHAT we don't want is a big mistake that I have witnessed many people make, including myself in the past. It's natural! Of course, it is important to get clear on WHAT you are moving away from and to get clear on the obstacles.

But to create and consolidate new neural pathways and to reduce the connections of the old way of doing things you need to get clear on WHAT you DO want.

The best approach for achieving commitment from ourselves and others who are learning new skills and changing habits is to dream; to imagine all possible outcomes and then to get really clear on specifically WHAT we want to do differently as tangibly and specifically as possible (and then take step by step action!).

What If I Find It Difficult to Use Visualisation?

Many people can visualise easily and can use it to work quickly and effectively on chosen topics. Nevertheless, not everyone is naturally good at visualisation and some find it very frustrating and challenging.

As far back as 1932, Bartlett[34] (one of the first psychologists to relate memory performance to how people learn) found that he could classify his research participants based on their informal comments as either:

> **Visualisers**, who claimed to rely mainly upon visual imagery; or

> **Vocalisers**, who claimed to rely mainly upon language cues rather than mental images.

Since Bartlett started researching this area, we now know that most people have both abilities but to slightly different degrees. So, if you cannot visualise something, you could try vocalising it, in detail regarding the specifics and the tangibles.

I'd like to tell you about Erika Brodnock who found visualisation very challenging, but found a way to make it work for herself.

I first met Erika, a multi-award-winning entrepreneur and coach, many years ago when she was developing her company: Karisma Kidz. She had a mission to help children develop Emotional Intelligence. But like many of us, even though she had attended numerous courses to develop herself personally and in business, she was still getting stuck in some old behavioural patterns.

Erika told me that any time she tried visualising, she closed her eyes and all she saw was darkness, with a hint of red if there was a light source in the room. She would listen as others described all the wonderful things they could see in their mind's eye and how these made them feel.

When she closed her eyes, she saw nothing, no matter how many times someone told her, "It's easy, we can all do it!". She was offered the explanation that the pictures in her mind were moving too fast, but that didn't work either. She still couldn't see anything. The more she tried, the less she saw.

She felt downright irritated. But she was determined not to give up on her quest to see the pictures in her mind, in order to 'visualise' the version of her she wanted to exist, because she was aware of many successful people who swore by it and all the research findings behind visualisation.

The eventual breakthrough for her was the process of using her strongest sense: hearing. When she vocalised a description of WHAT she wanted to create, the pictures began to appear. If she said, "I can see the sea", the sea would appear.

She would then say, "I can see me", describe what she was wearing and how she looked, all inside her head, until the picture appeared exactly as she wished it to be.

After practicing this for a period of time she was able to close her eyes and see a picture as she wanted it to appear.

If your strongest sense is feeling, then feeling your way to the picture with various sensations will work effectively too.

Just keep in mind that 'visualisation' can include any of the senses. They can be visual (images and pictures), kinaesthetic (how the body feels), or auditory (the applause of a crowd).

Using the mind, we can call up these images repeatedly, enhancing the skill through repetition or rehearsal, similar to physical practice.

Certain schools of thought in psychology and more and more evidence in the crossover between neuroscience and change find that the brain does not process things logically with words and numbers. It has been argued that the language of our unconscious mind and of creating real change is sight, sound, smell, taste and feeling. Feeling it can include sensations such as tingling hands or warm feet, otherwise known as interoception, Feeling will also include paying attention to our autonomic system, for example how our breathing would be in this situation, or whether our heart feels like it will be beating faster or slower. Feeling into it also includes proprioception, which is our ability to perceive the position and movement of our body.

What this means, is that 'thinking' about it is not enough. If we want to speed up consolidation, we need to 'feel' it. Visualisation is a whole-body phenomenon.

Athletes, business leaders and scientists have proven time and time again that visualisation and mental practice works! Please remember that you also need to practice the new behaviour for real! Physically performing the new skill alongside visualising yourself carrying out this new behaviour and imagining the neural connections will work quicker and more effectively in forming the new habit than just performing the behaviour alone or just thinking about it.

Follow the **Step 1: CLARITY: WHAT?** questions below about the change you want to make and then proceed to the visualisation exercise.

STEP 1: CLARITY: WHAT?

1) WHAT do you want to do differently? (Get as specific as you can)

2) Transfer from above to here:

"When it comes to _____(the new WHAT), I'm the type of person who _____".

Does this align with the thing you want to do differently? If not, what work do you need to do with your self-identity or what support do you need to put in place to overcome the old habitual self-identity?

3) WHAT is each step involved with doing the new behaviour?

4) WHAT does each step of the new behaviour being enacted look / feel / sound / taste / smell like?

5) WHAT does the outcome being achieved look / feel / sound / taste / smell like?

Note: If you prefer to print out a version of the worksheets with the questions for all steps, rather than write in this book, please see **www.adaptastraining.com/books**.

A Visualisation Exercise

To speed up the process of changing your habits, try the following:

Decide WHAT your new habit is going to be.

Sit back or lie down, making sure you are comfortable.

Close your eyes.

Take five nice big deep breaths, breathing in through your nose and out through your mouth. As you breathe in, focus on your stomach, abdomen, lower back and waist expanding and filling with air (so that the inhale is not coming high into your chest, potentially sending you into fight or flight). As you breathe out, feel your body softening and letting go of tension.

Scan your body from the top of your head down to your feet. Feel the contact between your body and the chair or the floor. Does it feel heavy? Where is the heaviest point of contact? Feel your hands and your feet on the floor. Allow everything to relax.

Now, imagine you are performing your new habit. Will you be placing vegetables in to a pot as you cook a healthy meal? Will you be pumping sweat and feeling energised at a gym? Will you be having more regular feedback conversations with the individuals in your team to create a high performing team?

As you get that image really clear in your mind, hear the sounds you are hearing, feel the feelings you are feeling:

Interoception – for example, tingling in your feet, warm hands.

Proprioception – your body moving in space or complete stillness and balance.

Autonomic – heart beating, tense or relaxed muscles, breath slowing down or speeding up.

See, hear and feel everything that goes with performing this new habit as if you are really in the situation (not just watching the situation!). Take as long to do the new habit in your mind as it would if you were doing it in real life.

Now, once you are vividly imagining that experience, start to run it faster and faster until you feel all the feelings (as above) that come with having that new habit.

As you run through the experience, imagine the neurons throughout your brain firing and connecting. Imagine the neurons passing their electrical charge along to each other. See neural pathways being formed that represent the new habit.

Do this exercise every day for a week, repeating the visualisation and the imagining of the experience of the event, with the neurons firing and creating pathways throughout your brain. Imagine that experience and the pathways being created 10, 15 or 20 times in one sitting.

> *Your breathing is your greatest friend. Return to it in all your troubles and you will find comfort and guidance.*
>
> Unknown[35]

STEP 2: CURIOSITY: WHY?

Don't wait until everything is just right. It will never be perfect. There will always be challenges, obstacles and less than perfect conditions. So what? Get started now. With each step you take, you will grow stronger and stronger, more and more skilled, more and more self-confident and more and more successful.

Mark Victor Hansen[36]

Now that you are really clear on the specific WHAT, it's time to think about your WHY. I argued with myself about whether WHAT or WHY would come first in this process because without WHY there is often no point in moving to WHAT. However, please remember I mentioned earlier that these seven steps can be followed consecutively, simultaneously and continuously. You will know what works best for YOU!

There are three main items that can be considered regarding the WHY to creating real and lasting change:

> **Firstly**, pondering on WHY you want to make this change or learn something new.

> **Secondly**, distinguishing between motivation and discipline.

> **Thirdly**, connecting with the values that are most important to you in life.

This section will help you start thinking more about the WHY of your WHAT.

WHY You Want This Change

Our WHY is very important to keeping motivation up. When we are not clear on our motivation and our WHY, for the majority of us, our focus and our performance declines.

For example, WHY do you want to listen more effectively? Is it to retain your best people? Or to make people feel heard? Is it to develop better working relationships and maybe other relationships too?

Or WHY do you want to do three sessions of exercise each week or eat more fruit and vegetables? Is it to have more energy throughout every day? Or to feel stronger in your body to take up surfing? Or to keep up with your fit and active children?

You may recall in **Part 1**, I mentioned that to learn and create change as adults we need to really focus. It needs to feel urgent and we've got to increase some of the chemicals of learning in our brain and body. This focus and urgency can evolve from clarity on our WHY.

Get clear on your specific WHY. WHY do you want to do it for YOU? Make sure your WHY is not just for somebody else. If you do that, your motivation will only last so long. If you can connect with the feeling of your WHY , as well as logically, you will engage not only the goal-oriented more recently-evolved parts of the brain but also more systems within the brain and body. The more systems within the brain and body involved, the more focus, motivation and discipline that ensues.

On attending the leadership programme, Catherine initially stated that she wanted to improve her communication because she had been told by her own line manager that he would like her to move into his role as he wanted to make a move cross-functionally. He was looking for a change and new challenge for himself. Catherine did not see herself in his role but she was honoured that he recommended her to go on this programme. So, when I asked Catherine to share her WHY, it was actually her line manager's WHY that she shared.

She soon realised that she had to do some thinking on her own WHY to create the focus required. By the end of Session 1, she got there. As far back as school, she had been left out of teams because she didn't put herself forward, or offer up her opinion, because she thought her ideas were stupid. These days she knew her ideas were useful and appreciated by her colleagues, and that's why she had continued to be promoted. But she was still holding back in certain situations, especially with more assertive team members, and with senior colleagues. On this leadership programme, she decided once and for all that she was going to become a more assertive, impactful and influential individual because she knew she had way more to offer and could go a lot further in her career quickly, if she worked on this competency. When she got clear on her own WHY, she could feel the excitement at being able to stand her ground, regardless of what level her colleague was at.

Motivation is a key factor in learning and habit change. You could view motivation as a cycle where thoughts influence behaviours, and behaviours then drive action and performance.

This inner drive to behave or act in a certain manner is the force that causes us to change our desires into actual achievements. Most of us can recognise the feelings that go with being motivated: focused, in flow, passionate, excited, driven.

And most of us know the feelings that go with having no motivation; bored, listless, apathetic, sluggish, distracted.

Incidentally, this is one reason neurorehabilitation after brain injury can be so difficult. One of the most common deficits after Traumatic Brain Injury (TBI) is a lack of motivation (typically after frontal or thalamic damage), so TBI patients can be less motivated to engage with rehabilitation approaches. If you have not experienced a TBI, make the most of your natural ability to feel motivated. It is something many of us take for granted!

WHY: Distinguishing Between Motivation and Discipline

Motivation is just not enough. If you are going to commit to making changes in your life, then it requires dedication, discipline and practice to create lasting change. The brain is plastic and can change, but repetition is the key to consolidating stronger neural connections to create and consolidate long-term change. We all know that motivation only lasts so long. Repetition will only occur if you are motivated and ultimately once the motivation fades, it's going to take discipline.

Getting clear on our WHY, helps us to create discipline to keep on track.

Consider whether your WHY is towards what you want ('the carrot') or away from what you don't want ('the stick')?

When learning something new or creating a new habit, are you motivated by:

"What can I gain, by creating this new behaviour or skill?"
or

"What do I stand to lose by not creating it?"

By asking yourself what you have to gain or lose, you will help your brain and body to filter information and be crystal clear on your WHY.

WHY is it worth putting the effort in? What difference will it make to your life? We need to get clear on 'WHY' we want to do it; to gain something or to not lose something. In **Part I**, we considered 'loss aversion'; our strong preference for minimising losses over acquiring gains. So, work out what you stand to lose by not doing something differently, as well as working out what you want to gain. This will give you a number of 'WHYs' and ultimately in my experience, most of us need to move toward the gains quickly, to create the discipline required.

My colleague Alistair McBride puts it well:

> *Back in our evolutionary past when we saw a venomous snake, how motivated were we to get away from it on a scale of 1 to 10? Probably 9 or 10, right? We sprint away and we can see it in the distance, it's not chasing us. What happens to our motivation? It goes down. The further away from the threat, the greater the dip in motivation. This is why away from goals can be a great motivator in the very short term and at the start of a goal, but you quickly need to have a pull or toward motivator to keep your motivation. When you are running a long race and turn a corner, in the distance you finally see the finish line. Does your motivation go down, stay the same, or go up? For most people it will go up because you realise 'there's the line, that's my goal that I've been working toward'.*

What is the WHY that will assist you in creating the discipline?

Let's be clear, the bottom line is: If you don't have a WHY, and are not motivated to learn enough to create the discipline required, then consolidation is unlikely to take place.

I was told earlier last year by an orthopaedic surgeon that I needed a hip replacement. I had been experiencing pain in that area but that was the last thing I expected to be told at my age. I sought out a number of other opinions and options. My physiotherapist had for over a year been urging me to do Pilates. Feeling desperate, I finally gave it a go. Within two weeks of attending Reformer Pilates three times per week, most of the pains I was experiencing dissipated! The fear of a hip replacement motivated me to try out something that had been recommended to me by a professional and that I had been putting off! I continued to attend for another two weeks and couldn't believe how much stronger I felt in such a short space of time. But once the fear of "What do I stand to lose? – just my hip!" disappeared, I was no longer motivated to go to the classes as regularly. And then I went on a trip to the USA. No Pilates and no pain for the whole three weeks. However, two days after returning home, the pains returned. Again, I was motivated to attend Pilates by my fear of losing my original hip. It got me back to the classes and again within two weeks I felt great! Once more at this point, the motivation and discipline were waning. It was time-consuming getting to the classes, and I had better things to do with my time, like run a business and finish this book!

I had to focus on what could I gain. So, my focus became strengthening my body up through Pilates for a trip I was planning to make in four months' time that would involve a lot of walking and other physical activity. This got me future focused, with a flight booked to work towards. We all know what happened then. Covid-19 hit. The planned trip was no more. However, I got straight on to zoom Pilates classes and now it has become part of my weekly morning routine because I got clear on my WHY. I found the motivation towards that and hence created the discipline which I then managed to maintain even though the carrot disappeared. I have now been successfully attending three Pilates sessions virtually every week for many months and am genuinely feeling the benefit of it. I can't imagine my life any more without Pilates and just wish I had started it earlier. I have created long-lasting change.

WHY and Values

Understand your WHY and you'll be able to regulate your behaviour better initially. If you can identify a personal need or want, or a reason to make a change, and connect this to the process of change, then you will be more motivated to stick to the plan. It's worth spending some time considering what motivates you around this specific change.

One of the most powerful techniques I have seen work for myself and my own clients is considering the values we hold dear.

What are YOUR core values? Your values are the things that you believe are important in the way you live and work. Values are basic and fundamental beliefs that guide or motivate attitudes or actions. Values describe the personal qualities you choose to embody to guide your actions; the sort of person you want to be; the manner in which you treat yourself and others, and your interaction with the world around you. They provide the general guidelines for conduct. They determine your priorities, and, deep down, they're probably the measures you use to tell if your life is turning out the way you want it to. When the things that you do and the way you behave match your values, life is usually good – you're satisfied and content. But when these don't align with your personal values, that's when things feel .. . wrong. This can be a real source of unhappiness.

The values that are important to you might include hard work, fun, diligence, openness, love, grit, perfection, faith, service, dependability, perseverance, beauty, pleasure, accountability, commitment, dependability, serenity, dignity, honesty, responsibility, sincerity, accomplishment, competence, adventure, credibility, knowledge, determination, skilfulness, loyalty, determination, creativity. These are just a few examples from hundreds of potential values you might hold.

For example, a client of mine was recently struggling to have some conversations she needed to have with colleagues. Many circumstances had changed in the organisation within which she was working. This had impacted on her confidence and she had fallen into the habit of not speaking her mind at meetings or sharing her ideas on the future of her department and the organisation.

By identifying with her values of honesty and compassion, she found it easier to find the confidence to start the process of having these conversations to speak her mind and moving back into the mode of sharing her ideas at meetings.

For myself, identifying and connecting consciously with my value of freedom, especially when I feel myself falling foul of the change I want to make, has helped me create the discipline of attending the virtual Pilates classes, even when it's the last thing I feel like doing!

Can you connect your WHY to one of your top values?

Follow the **Step 2: CURIOSITY: WHY?** questions below about the change you want to make using your tangible WHAT.

... when I first started working with Tracy [personal trainer], finding motivation was hard. She advised me to think of exercise as an automatic routine, no different from brushing your teeth, to avoid getting distracted. Now it is part of my life – I exercise Monday to Friday at 10am and always stick with it.

Dove (2019), citing Gwyneth Paltrow[37]

STEP 2: CURIOSITY: WHY?

1)   WHY do you want to do it?

2)   What can you gain, by creating this new behaviour or skill?

3) What do you stand to lose by not creating this new behaviour or skill?

4) Write down several positive aspects associated with completing your goal for YOURSELF.

5) Focus on the most positive aspects. How do they look, sound, smell, taste and feel (including limbs, heartbeat, breath, etc).

6) Now that you have thought about your own WHY, write down several positive aspects associated with completing your goal

for others (family, colleagues, friends, the world!) involved. For some of us this will also help our motivation and discipline.

7) Focus on the most positive aspects associated with completing your goal for others. How do they look, sound and feel?

8) Are there any values that are important to you, that you can make your WHY connect with? Examples of values might be honesty, integrity, compassion, happiness, freedom, and there are many more. (See Book 1, *Our Learning Brain*, for more discussion and a useful exercise to utilise to get clarity on your top values).

9) How can this WHY become part of your daily or weekly routine to create discipline?

Note: If you prefer to print out a version of the worksheets with the questions for all steps, rather than write in this book, please see **www.adaptastraining.com/books**.

A Motivational Exercise

We've all experienced ambivalence to change. Change can feel like too much effort and as we know, the brain and body are on the lookout to keep us safe and protect us from change!

Motivational Interviewing (MI) is used to elicit behaviour change by helping people to explore and resolve ambivalence to change. Even though this method is generally used by medical practitioners with patients who are ambivalent to change, it's worth considering the main facets of MI with yourself for all types of learning and habit change, especially if you are getting really stuck in old patterns and challenged with doing things differently.

MI was initially coined by William Miller in 1983,[38] and it has been applied to a number of areas of behavioural change. There are multiples of research papers backing up its efficacy (Martins & McNeil, 2009).[39]

MI uses a guiding style to engage with patients, clarify their strengths and aspirations, evoke their own motivations for change, and promote autonomy of decision making.

The philosophy of MI is that people approach change with varying levels of readiness. With this approach, the role of the medical practitioner is to assist patients and clients to become more aware of the implications of change and / or of not changing through a non-judgemental interview in which clients do most of the talking. This is useful to consider, because most of us judge ourselves to some degree, and once the judgement starts and the limiting beliefs are rampant, change is unlikely! And as we know it's going to be useful to talk to ourselves to visualise things as we want them to be, not as we don't want them to be.

You can use many of the main facets of MI with yourself:

> **Empathy** – we can be hard on ourselves. Acknowledge how you are feeling. If you are finding it tough, don't berate yourself. Just acknowledge the feelings and remind yourself you are human. Try to be kind to yourself in making change. To help yourself, you could break it down into achievable parts rather than trying to do everything at once! Tiny changes over time eventually compound to monumental change. Some examples:
>
>> Planning your week ahead EVERY Friday afternoon, over a few months will enable you to get more done,

and make you more effective with your time than working late into the night two nights per week!

Doing 10 minutes of resistance exercise using your own body weight every morning or every second morning will build your core and strength more effectively than making it to the gym once per week for 1.5 hours!

Working out the gap between your goal and your current behaviour. This is one of the very basics of coaching. You can be your own best coach. What is the gap between your current behaviour and where you want to be? As above, break it down and work out the smaller steps to bridge that gap. Take one step at a time and eventually it will compound.

Examine all the different viewpoints (any one of us can have many viewpoints on one goal or aspiration, and many points of resistance). Motivation is rarely enhanced past a few days by anything that is not internal. It doesn't matter how convincing someone or something else is initially. It's got to come from inside you. Get to know your different viewpoints on the matter. I've mentioned the stories we tell ourselves and the limiting beliefs we hold previously. Get to know your stories and then learn to work with them and manage them.

Focus on current achievements and strengths to grow our self-efficacy. What are some skills / strengths or past successes that might let you know you can do this? For example:

Do you want to improve your presentation skills, to become more engaging and impactful, but find it challenging to put yourself forward to give presentations for fear of messing up? Consider your strengths in light of yourself as a communicator in general. Are you great at building new relationships in your work and personal life? Learning to be a great presenter is just another mode of creating great relationships. If you are focused on getting to know your audience and giving them value, or something useful to think about, then this is really 90% of what you need to be a great presenter.

Was there a time when you went for a run every morning and felt great because of it? But then you got into couch-hogging habits because of an injury or because you were exhausted from the expectation and busyness of life? You know you did it before, so focus on that and work out how you can do it again. If you can't run anymore because of an injury there are many other things that you could do. Get a bicycle, go swimming, or do Pilates classes. I am Pilates' newest and biggest fan, you can tell! These activities are not as boring or as simple as you might think. Try a few different things out until you find the thing you enjoy!

STEP 3: FEELING AWARENESS: HOW?

Have the sections on 'WHAT' and 'WHY' given you enough to think about and work with?

If you are following the Seven Step process, is it helping you get clarity on changing your habit or embedding some new learning?

Nobody said it was going to be easy. If it was easy, we'd all be changing habits successfully all the time. And there would be no need for people and teams to work with people like me and my peers.

Whether you are applying change to your own life and work or are looking to support others in change, the HOW is a little more challenging. HOW is all about feeling awareness which is less simple to manage in ourselves and others than the WHAT and WHY.

We will explore the importance of 'HOW' on our ability to learn and change. Once again, there are three ways of getting the HOW working for us in creating change and learning new skills:

> **Firstly**, considering whether you are more predisposed towards positive or negative thinking and feeling.

> **Secondly**, examining whether you have a habit of practicing gratitude.

> **Thirdly**, reflecting on whether you make change and learning safe, or even fun for yourself (and others).

These items will hopefully give you a lot to think about for yourself as the learner, whilst also considering others whom you are working with or leading.

HOW? Positive *versus* Negative Thinking

Did you wake up today feeling good about yourself, the day and life in general? Or did you wake up thinking, "Here we go again", "I hate getting out of bed" or "I hate my job"?

HOW do you feel about yourself and your life? Are you negative, unhappy, de-motivated, or positive, happy, and motivated?

HOW you feel has an impact on your ability to learn and change habits.

'HOW' refers to your feeling awareness. Feeling awareness is the ability to recognise and make sense of HOW you are feeling. Feeling awareness is being able to recognise how you feel and then make choices on how you respond and behave. Many people discuss 'emotions' as 'feelings'. Emotions can actually create rigidity in our lives. By viewing our feelings as hard and fast emotions, we give ourselves little choice as to how we feel. However as referred to in the WHAT section, there are many different aspects to how we feel, including the feelings associated with the sense of the internal state of the body, the autonomic nervous system and the sense though which we perceive the position and movement of our body. By paying attention to these feelings and working with them, we bring more fluidity into how we respond and behave, and of course how we learn and change habits.

If you have read Barbara Fredrickson's book *Positivity*[40] or Maureen Gaffney's book *Flourishing*,[41] you will have come across the 3:1 and 5:1 ratio.

Fredrickson's research shows that we need three positives for every one negative in our thoughts, experiences and feelings, to survive. Gaffney says we need five positives for every one negative to thrive and flourish in life and that:

> *If the ratio falls below 3:1, and stays down, you are tipped into a downward spiral from which it is hard to escape. This is when someone becomes depressed; when a relationship enters a new, destructive state; or when a team or an organisation becomes dysfunctional.*

When you feel good, thinking, making decisions and taking action in pursuing goals requires less effort. When you feel positive, you are more likely to be able to recall good memories.

When you feel negative, things couldn't get much worse for your memory. Not only are you more likely to access more negative memories or thoughts, but these negativities get in the way of accessing positive memories and thoughts. In turn this can interfere with getting those endorphins, dopamine and other chemicals increasing or decreasing in the way we need them to.

Mark Williams, the snooker player, tells how he missed an easy pot, and to stop himself from ruminating about it, he recited song lyrics over and over in his head until it was his turn to play again. He distracted himself from dwelling on the mistake and, as a result, he didn't repeat it.

This approach is also used in neurorehabilitation, in a technique called Error-free Learning. People with brain injury are trained to do a task (for example, make a cup of tea) very slowly, perfectly, over and over again, without ever making a mistake. It's known that making an error will lead to rumination, which slows recovery.

Brain plasticity is a two-way street. Unwanted bad habits or feelings continue because the brain has wired itself through years of repeated behaviour and experiences. We must literally tell our brain how we want to feel, and not what we don't want to feel! As discussed previously, to create change, we must literally rewire the brain! We can drive brain change positively or negatively.

For example, there is a story that is often associated with famous performers such as Bruce Springsteen. Apparently, Bruce has shared that in the past that when he was backstage about to perform, he felt extremely nervous. He felt nauseous and would perspire heavily. However, at some point in his career, he realised that his body responded similarly whether he was nervous or excited. He eventually made the decision that until he felt he was nauseous and was perspiring heavily, he was not ready to step onto the stage and give his fans they best show of their lives. He recognised the feelings in his body, and instead of associating them with nervousness, he associated them with excitement.

This is something that resonates with me, as I used to feel nauseous and perspire heavily before speaking to a group of people. Not only did I feel nauseous, but I would not be able to sleep or eat for two or three days before doing so and would also berate myself for not knowing enough or not preparing enough, even though I had prepared three times too much information. At a certain point in my career, through a process of working with my thoughts and feelings, over time I got to a point where I stopped giving myself a rough time. I now have similar feelings in my body but because I associate it all with excitement, I can sleep and eat and I enjoy the experience of facilitating and delivering learning experiences with groups of people and at events. I feel excited rather than nervous.

Make no mistake about it. Bad habits are called 'bad habits' for a reason. They kill our productivity and creativity. They slow us down. They hold us back from achieving our goals. And they're detrimental to our health.

John Rampton[42]

It's up to you which way you want to wire your brain, towards the negative or towards the positive: Towards the "I can do" *versus* "I can't do", towards the "I am a victim of circumstances" *versus* "I am the master of my own universe". In every moment of every day, we have a choice. We often just don't realise it, because our unconscious and well-established routines exert so much control over how we feel and how we behave.

One of the things I notice when working with individuals and groups is that many people don't realise they have a CHOICE. We get stuck in ruts, we believe we are victims of our surroundings, martyrs to our choices, or at the mercy of our genes. Indeed, I was put on antidepressants many times as a teenager and in my 20s. It wasn't until I realised that I could focus my thoughts in a different direction and I built in daily routines and exercises to manage my thoughts and feelings that I realised just how much choice and control I had. I am not saying that antidepressants didn't serve me earlier in my life or that they will not be useful to many people, and save lives. But they are not the only approach. Sadly, many doctors will only offer you the quick fix! And many of us want the quick fix and are not willing to move into the uncomfortable feelings that go with doing things differently or trying new things out. It's natural. If I haven't stated it enough – our brain and body are working hard to keep us safe and that means doing things as we have always done them, and feeling like we have always felt. If we want to do something a different way, we need to get comfortable with feeling uncomfortable.

Here is one very simple technique that, if practiced every day, will compound to make you feel more focused on "I can do" in life to impact on your 'HOW'. So simple, you might just laugh it off!

'HOW' Practicing Gratitude

> *Cultivate the habit of being grateful for every good thing that comes to you, and to give thanks continuously. And because all things have contributed to your advancement, you should include all things in your gratitude.*
>
> Ralph Waldo Emerson[43]

At the outset of this section, I mentioned that feeling awareness is the ability to recognise and make sense of HOW you are feeling, and then make choices on how you respond and behave.

Practicing gratitude brings focus to how you feel and gets you focused on feeling better. Research over the past two decades in Positive Psychology,[44] repeatedly finds that those who remind themselves every day what they are grateful for are happier, more positive, more resilient, have higher openness to their feelings, ideas, and values, have greater competence and achievement striving, and have more environmental mastery (the ability to choose or change the surrounding context using physical or mental actions, as well as being able to control events).

What can you do to practice gratitude?

A number of approaches have been found to increase gratitude, and hence resilience, well-being, happiness etc. Here are three of them:

Daily listing of things for which to be grateful.

Behavioural expressions of gratitude;

Philanthropy.

1) Daily listing of things for which to be grateful

This is the one I do every day and that I recommend to all my clients. Every morning when I wake up, I consider and write down three things I am grateful for. You could also do it at night instead, directly before bed, as a grateful mind sleeps better according to research! Research has found that the benefits to well-being from doing this exercise for three to four weeks are still observed six months later!

> *What we found was something as simple as writing down three things you're grateful for every day for 21 days in a row significantly increases your level of optimism and it holds for the next six months. The research is amazing. It proves we actually can change.*
>
> Stillman (2016), citing Shawn Achor[45]

The most impactful way to do it is to think of three different things each day. Repeating the same things day in, day out, will enable your brain to habituate to or disengage from the exercise, and so you will not reap the benefits. I promise you won't run out of things. It could be over-arching elements of your life like, 'I am grateful for my health' or 'I am grateful for my family' to specifics such as, 'I am so grateful for having fingers that work', 'I am grateful for this warm blanket on my bed', 'I am grateful for that dream I just had'. You won't run out of things ever, if you engage your mind and body in the process.

As Maureen Gaffney[46] states:

> *It's easy to be grateful when things are going well and you are in a good mood. But it is when things are going badly and you are in a negative mood that gratitude is most important. Flourishing people seem to have the knack of being able to appreciate over and over again the good things in their lives and as a consequence to feel that their lives are fulfilling, meaningful, and productive.*

2) Behavioural expressions of gratitude: The gratitude visit

Write a gratitude letter (of at least 300 words) to a living person who has been a positive influence in your life or who did something nice for you, and then call to them in person or video call them and read it aloud to them.

People who have done this exercise report more positive feelings and less depression at the immediate post-test, one month and three-month follow-ups.[47] The effect of this on people's well-being is very large.

The long-term impact of the gratitude visit is not however as strong as the gratitude lists. So, I say, why not do a gratitude visit every two months or so, as well as your daily gratitude lists for a double whammy?!

3) Philanthropy

Do something philanthropic – in other words, help others. For example, a local charity, something where people are in need. Researchers find measurable differences in the level and quality of happiness obtained from philanthropic actions versus activities that were considered "fun". And the effect lasts.

American psychologist, educator and author, Martin Seligman, and his colleagues, for recent decades have studied happiness. In his book, *Authentic Happiness*, he states:[48]

> *In the lab, children and adults who are happy display more empathy ... When we are happy, we are less self-focused, we like others more, and we want to share our good fortune even with strangers. When we are down, though, we become distrustful, turn inward, and focus defensively on our own needs.*

By doing more for those in need, we become more grateful for what we have, and the result is that we feel better about our lives.

Either way, training yourself to adopt a grateful outlook as your primary response can be one of the most constructive habits you ever develop. Both positive and negative events can lead to gratitude, with the negative ones helping us appreciate what we already have. Gratitude involves deliberate choice, as with all techniques shared in this book, and requires discipline to make it stick, like any other good habit.

Gratitude will get your brain focused on the positive aspects of your life and will pull you towards the modes of operating that you know will help you to be more effective. Practicing gratitude has been shown time and time again in numerous studies to be the one thing that can make us happier and more focused on the positive potential in our lives.

> *When you are grateful, fear disappears and abundance appears.*
>
> Anthony Robbins[49]

60

'HOW' Psychological Safety and Fun

Psychological Safety

Long-term change is enhanced by behaviour and circumstances. Learning occurs with focused attention, but as mentioned many times, it can be inhibited by any block to accepting new experiences – for example, feeling unsafe or unsupported in the change.

Have you heard of the term 'Psychological Safety'? This term refers to the degree to which people view an environment as accepting and conducive to interpersonally-risky behaviours like speaking up, asking for help, asking questions, sharing concerns and admitting mistakes.

Creating psychological safety requires feeling awareness – the ability to recognise and make sense of other people's feelings, as well as our own. This is highly important if we are going to support others in change.

> *High psychological safety can catalyse a positive self-fuelling cycle for adult development and how an individual engages in their environment affects their ability to adapt and grow.*
>
> *Edmondson et al. (2016)[50]*

Studies show that psychological safety allows for moderate risk-taking, speaking our mind, creativity, and sticking our neck out without fear of being slapped down.

Psychological safety plays a vital role in the 'HOW', helping people overcome barriers to learning and change in interpersonally-challenging work environments. It also impacts on the wider context – for example, the performance of teams; the highest performing teams create and maintain psychological safety.

Perhaps you have heard of Project Aristotle?[51] Google wanted to know why some teams excelled while others fell behind. They had an assumption, like many of us would, that if you put the best people together, they would be the best team. They studied 180 Google teams, conducted 200+ interviews, and analysed over 250 different team attributes.

However, one of the main characteristics of the most effective teams that transpired was psychological safety. Google found that teams with psychologically safe environments had employees who were less likely to leave, more likely to harness the power of diversity, and were more successful.

Consider the importance of this, especially if you are working in a position with responsibility for other people's learning and development. Whether you are a team leader, a line manager, or a learning and development specialist, this is you!

We have discussed motivation earlier in this book. Even when people are motivated to change, perceptions associated with the risk of such change may inhibit their ability to act on their motivations.[52] And as we know, in a busy organisation, there isn't always time outside of core activities to give focus to this.

This is one of the areas that our manager from the leadership programme, Jim, missed out on. He was so used to telling people that they were doing things wrong and fixing things for them and hence disempowering them that he neither created a feeling of psychological safety or helped them to make the changes that they needed in order to grow.

When our ideas are dismissed, by ourselves or by others, or we are reprimanded for doing something wrong, or when we are humiliated in any way, we go into fight or flight. As discussed in **Part 1**, our amygdala responds immediately and takes over our reactions. The System 1, 'act now rather than think it through' takes over. In doing so, System 2, the higher brain functions go into lazy mode, and thus our creativity, openness to new experiences, ability to think strategically and trying alternative ways of doing things shuts down.

Whereas, when we keep the higher order brain functions involved, we remain in a mode of openness and creativity and our ability to have a sense of humour and to be curious increases! This all impacts on our 'HOW'.

Fun

We all know that when we are having fun, everything seems easier. Many people take up running with a running group, or musical instrument classes with a group, or get involved with corporate social responsibility (CSR) in their organisation, because it is more fun to share the experience with others as well as feeling accountable to showing up.

Combining extensive research and case studies from some of the world's most successful organisations, bestselling author Adrian Gostick and humourist Scott Christopher[53] discuss HOW humour in the workplace has many benefits. In their book, *The Levity Effect: Why it Pays to Lighten Up*, they find that humour:

> Helps build camaraderie.
>
> Increases productivity.
>
> Enhances employee satisfaction and loyalty.
>
> Encourages creativity and innovation for a better workplace and bigger profits.

Where there is fun, there is creativity. Incorporating fun and humour helps people relax and feel safe and secure in the work environment. When this happens, people perform better, think better, and are comfortable enough to share their most creative ideas without fearing embarrassment.

Remember when you were a young child, you played all the time? You gained invaluable learning and skills through playing. But mainstream education gradually switches the emphasis from playing to passively sitting and listening. Into adulthood, fun is often missing from our days and in many workplaces.

Of course, fun and creativity are experienced differently by all of us, so be cautious not to make assumptions here! There isn't just one prescription for fun and enjoyment for everyone. Our experience of fun also can change based on experiences we find ourselves in, and the people we are surrounded by.

Humans are social beings who thrive through connectedness with other humans. The brain is a social organ, innately designed to learn through shared experiences. Brains grow best in this context of interactive discovery and through the co-creation of stories that shape and support memories of what is being learned. Evidence from the field of neuroscience shows that we require positive social interaction and nurturance in order to learn.[52] Even rats housed alone compared to those in groups show differences in performance on tasks.

A safe, trusting environment will support people to get in the mood and find themselves having fun when they least expect it.

Dorothy Billington, author of *Life is an Attitude: How to Grow Forever Better*,[54] has run studies on why some men and women continue to grow as long as they live – while others do not. For example, she has studied English-as-Second-Language classes for new immigrants, and comments that:

In classes where students feel safe, where lessons are focused on current language needs, where students are asked for input on what helps them most to learn, where students are actively involved in interesting and fun exercises, where there's lots of laughter and congeniality, students of all ages and backgrounds learn English fast and well. In classes where students are made to feel inadequate and threatened, little is learned.

She also comments:

These findings support the thinking of Malcolm Knowles (author of The Adult Learner: A Neglected Species[55]), who is recognised as the father of adult learning; his trailblazing work underlies many of our most effective adult education programs. He reminded us that in optimal adult learning programs, where adults learn best, both students and faculty also have fun, for it is exhilarating to really learn.

If you are at a loss as to HOW you can make habit change and learning for yourself and others more enjoyable, consider HOW something as simple as a smile can make a difference to HOW we feel and how we learn. Smiling triggers powerful feelings that can change our brain chemistry. Simply using the same muscles as smiling will put you in a better mood because use of those muscles is part of HOW the brain evaluates mood.[56]

Smiling creates what is termed a 'halo' effect that helps us remember events more vividly, while feeling more optimistic, more positive and more motivated.

Lewis (2005)[57]

Ultimately, a supportive environment is most conducive to open and productive engagement with learning and changing. People will rarely learn as much as they might in an environment that is not supportive. All of this impacts on HOW we feel and therefore on our learning and habit change.

STEP 3: FEELING AWARENESS: HOW?

Having considered your WHAT and WHY, now it's time to complete the HOW questions below:

1) What positively focused thoughts or questions do you need to practice to keep you on the right track?

2) HOW will you keep your thoughts about change positively focused rather than negatively focused?

3) HOW can you make this change fun? Or HOW can you make it feel safe?

4) If you were to take low-risk baby steps, what would these steps be?

5) What will you do to practice gratitude? How might this practice connect with what is possible for you in how you apply yourself to this new habit or learning ?

Note: If you prefer to print out a version of the worksheets with the questions for all steps, rather than write in this book, please see **www.adaptastraining.com/books**.

FEELING INTO THE HOW EXERCISE FOR A HABIT THAT FEELS NEGATIVE

Focusing on a new and positive habit helps break old habits. Firstly, identify a positive habit and congruent behaviour you would like to adopt.

Recognise the feelings in your body and mind:

> **Interoception** (the sense of the internal state of the body) – for example, warm hands, tingle in feet.

> **Proprioception** (the sense through which we perceive the position and movement of our body, including our sense of equilibrium and balance) – for example, balanced, stretching a limb.

> **Autonomic** (the autonomic nervous system regulates a variety of body processes that take place without conscious effort) – for example, breath becoming relaxed, heart beating, sweat.

Then identify the old habit you want to break.

Again, recognise the feelings in your body and mind. They might be a little different to the positive habit you want to adopt:

> **Interoception** (the sense of the internal state of the body) – for example, cold hands, hunger, pain.

> **Proprioception** (the sense through which we perceive the position and movement of our body, including our sense of equilibrium and balance) – for example, loss of balance, someone invading your personal space.

> **Autonomic** (the autonomic nervous system regulates a variety of body processes that take place without conscious effort) – for example, breath becoming shallower, heart beating, tense muscles.

Recognise other stimuli in your environment that occur just before you usually act on the negative habit (other people, emails, phone buzzing, etc). Instead of acting on the negative impulse, use your conscious attention to re-focus your thoughts and behaviours on the feelings of the new and positive habit you have identified. Substitute the new behaviour and feelings that are congruent with the positive habit you want to form in place of the behaviours and feelings of the

67

negative habit. Replace the old way of doing something with the new way, in mind and body. Then repeat, repeat, and repeat.

STEP 4: MEMORY: WHEN & WHERE?

Have you ever had the experience of promising yourself you are going to practice your listening skills, or delegate more, or timetable your week at the end of the previous week, or exercise more, or take your vitamins daily? Suddenly two weeks have gone by and you didn't do anything you had planned because you forgot! Memory is very important to understand and consider when making change, both for ourselves and for others.

It is important to get clear on your WHEN and WHERE right from the outset. WHEN and WHERE are you going to apply the new learning or make that change you've been meaning to make? You can engage your memory more actively rather than leaving things to chance. Learning and Memory go hand in hand.

> *Memory is a process of encoding, sorting and retrieving information.*
>
> *Carlson, Martin & Buskist* (2004)[58]

I invited guest author, Dr. Richard Roche to discuss memory and its impact on learning and habit change. Richard is the author of *Pioneering Studies in Cognitive Neuroscience* and *Why Science Needs Art: From Historical to Modern Day Perspectives*. Richard is fascinated with 'memory' in his teaching and in his research. We will discover why so much of what we learn does not stick.

In this chapter, we will learn:

Firstly, why attention given to information is so important if it's going to be remembered.

Secondly, some of the most important anatomical structures that are important for memory.

Thirdly, some tips on ways to make things memorable, looking at factors which influence memory both at the time of learning and later, at the recall stage.

A Lesson on Memory from Guest Author Dr. Richard Roche

Memory is central to almost everything we do – to who we are, our sense of self, our knowledge about the world, our ability to get from place to place, even being able to remember to do things that haven't yet happened, like pay a bill that's due next week. We rely on our memory all the time, yet the way we think about memory is often very different to the reality of what happens in our brains when we say we can 'remember' something.

In the laboratory, one of the main ways we can check if something has been learned is to check if a person (or mouse, or rat, or other animal) shows evidence of remembering it, whether it's a list of words, a face they've seen before, or a route through a maze. If we want to maximise learning potential, it's wise to know a bit about how memory works.

I'd like to invite you to look at memory in a bit of detail. By the end of this section on Memory, you'll hopefully think about memory – both your own and more generally – in a different way, and will have the knowledge to consider how memory is involved in habit change and more generally in learning. You will also have some ideas on ways to make your messages, content and / or communications more memorable when helping others to learn.

The Importance of Attention in Memory

Atkinson & Shiffrin (1968)[59] proposed a model, referred to as the *Multi-store or Modal model.* This model broke the structure of memory up into three types, based on duration:

> **Sensory Store** – most incoming information coming from the senses (vision, sound, touch, etc.) is retained here only for a few seconds. It is lost within a few seconds unless we pay particular attention to that sensation.

> **Short-Term / 'Working' Memory (STM***)* – if we pay particular attention to a sensation then the information is processed here. Information is retained as long as it is kept active – by thinking about the visual image, as if on a mental blackboard, or by repeating a new phone number or song lyric over and over again in a loop. Information can be kept alive in STM for 15 to 20 minutes.

70

Long-Term Memory (LTM) – if enough rehearsal of information takes place, it is then transferred into LTM, where facts and events can be retained for decades, even a lifetime.

Information cannot be retained, or make its way into our memories, if it is not first attended to. We are bombarded with a vast array of stimulation every day: sights, sounds, fact, tastes, experiences. Only a few will we remember, and for that to happen we first must pay attention.

In fact, we can look at something every day, maybe many times each day, and still not remember it. For example, which of these is the correct logo?

Google Google Google

Google Google Google

Figure 2: Google logo.

If you struggled with that, don't worry – it's a common problem. In 2015, Blake and colleagues published a study on UCLA students' ability to remember the iconic Apple logo.[60] When asked to draw the logo from memory, only one out of a class of 85 did so accurately. Then, when given a selection of logos to choose from, less than half the students (52 of whom were Apple users) were able to correctly identify the right one – you can try it yourself below.

The point is this; the process of memory cannot happen unless attention is first engaged. **Attention** is the first, and prerequisite, stage of the memory process.

Assuming attention has been engaged, the next stage of memory formation is **Encoding**. During encoding, the information is transformed into some code that the brain can use which will allow it to be retained.

71

Select the correct logo

Figure 3: Apple logo.

After encoding has taken place, the next stage – **Storage** – involves the information being maintained in the brain, sometimes for long periods of time.

Finally, when the memory is to be recalled, the stage of **Retrieval** takes place. This may sound very similar to what happens on a PC. You click Save on a file (encoding), it saves onto a hard disc, USB or cloud (storage). Later, when you open the file again, it appears in front of you (retrieval). And on the surface, that's true – but experimental studies into the nature of memory have revealed some interesting quirks of human memory that differ drastically from that of a computer. Specifically, they have shown that <u>conditions at the time of encoding and at the time of retrieval</u> can have a huge impact on the success of a memory being retained.

Cognitive psychologists in the 1970s, including Fergus Craik and Endel Tulving,[61] demonstrated the importance of factors at the time of encoding for memory formation. They showed that information was more likely to be remembered later if people had carried out more cognitive processing (or mental effort) on that material when they were learning it – for example, when shown word lists, people had better recall of the words if they imagined an image of each word (for example, eagle, mountain) compared to people who were told to focus on the font or case the words were written in (EAGLE or eagle). They found that the **depth of processing** at encoding had a major impact on subsequent recall.

Similarly, **elaboration** was also found to be important – people instructed to put each word from a list into an elaborate sentence (involving movement, action and imagery; for example, "*A great bird swooped down and carried off the struggling FISH*"). This type of sentence had better recall later compared to people who were told to just use a simple sentence ("*She cooked the FISH*").

Finally, a similar pattern was found for **distinctiveness:** unusual or distinctive words (such as those with a silent letter or non-phonetic pronunciation: *comb, yacht*) were better remembered than typical words (*tree, chair*).

Relate this to when you are learning something new and looking to create new habits – if you are not given the opportunity to practice what you are learning – that is, to elaborate and create depth of processing, immediately – then it is very difficult to retain, recall and use the information or skill as needed.

If you are in a role requiring others to change, which of these many ingredients, required to create real enduring memory, is not receiving thought, attention and time? Depth of processing? Elaboration? Distinctiveness? In the training of soft skills, quite often not enough thought is put into these aspects of memory.

Memory: The Anatomical Features

While there are two key brain areas – the prefrontal cortex (PFC) and the hippocampus – that appear crucial for memory, in fact a large portion of the brain is engaged when we remember something.

To explain this, think for a moment about what a memory really is – if you say that you can remember, for example, your last birthday party, you will be able to recall things like who was present (visual images of faces), what music was played (auditory imagery), what food and drink you had (gustatory), how you felt and a collection of other sensations associated with the occasion. So, in effect, the 'memory' you recall is a package of experiences in different sensory modalities. Now, research into sensory perception has shown that a very similar set of brain regions become activated when we experience and later remember sensory stimulation – that is, visual areas of occipital and temporal cortices light up when we perceive a visual stimulus (for example, a face), and a similar or overlapping set of structures become active when we remember that face. The same is true for the other senses. The areas active when we recall a tune are similar to those engaged when we hear a tune. So, what this means for memory is that, when we remember an event, we see reactivation in many of the same brain structures that were activated at the time of the original event – or, when we remember, we effectively re-live the event internally. That means we see large portions of the brain, visual, auditory, tactile and others, becoming activated when we remember something.

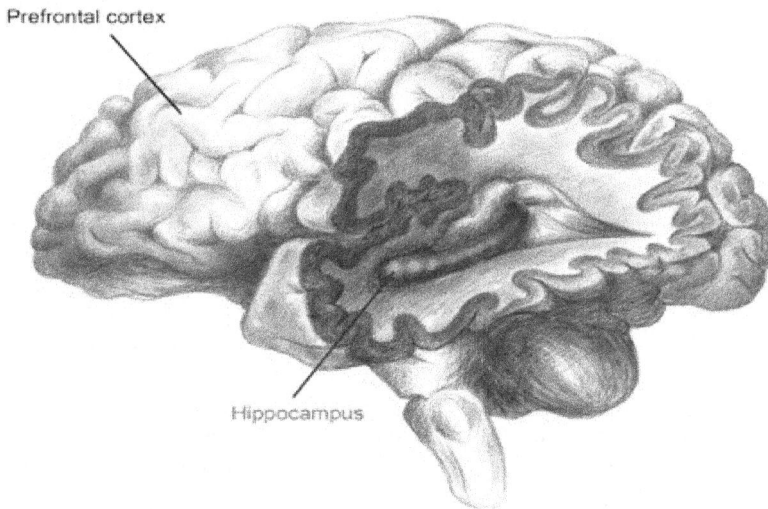

Prefrontal cortex

Hippocampus

Figure 4: Prefrontal cortex and hippocampus of the human brain.

In addition to this, the **prefrontal cortex** appears particularly important – we know that the PFC has a major role in STM, as we often observe impairments of STM in patients who have suffered frontal brain injury.

Brain imaging studies suggest that the left and right PFC have different roles in the different stages of memory; the right PFC is important for the retrieval stage of memory, while the left is activated during encoding.

The other crucial structure for memory is the **hippocampus**, a small arc of tissue which resembles a sea-horse. The hippocampus lies deep in the medial area of each temporal lobe.

Studies of brains with degenerative neurological diseases like dementia and Alzheimer's Disease show evidence that the hippocampus is among the first structures to suffer damage, supporting a role for hippocampus in encoding of new memories.

From this, we can conclude some important points about how the brain represents memories:

> Memories are represented by distributed brain circuits encompassing many different parts of the brain.

> The PFC and hippocampus have important and distinct roles in the processes of memory encoding and retrieval.

> When we remember something, what happens in our brain is effectively an internal re-living of the original event, with a similar collection of brain regions becoming activated as were engaged at the time of the experience itself. Therefore, the more we can engage the senses and the body in learning, the better for embedding it.

Think of memory *not* as a movie on a DVD – every time you play that DVD, the movie will be identical to the last time, and memory isn't like that. Rather, think of memory as being like going to see the same play on multiple nights – the play will always be the same, but the performance will vary from night to night, the nuances may change, actors may improvise or forget lines. So, every time we remember an event, that memory 'comes alive' and the performance begins anew. And because of this, with each act of remembering, thereby reactivating that brain circuit, we leave that memory open to modification. This is why our memories can be manipulated. Don't worry, this observation can be used for positive ends. Recently, this idea of modifying reactivated memories has been used to good effect with PTSD sufferers in helping them to cope with traumatic memories from war zones and other distressing environments.

For example, Celine and her team have been developing, with clients, Virtual Reality learning experiences to help people feel like they have dealt with customer objections or made it through difficult performance conversations, even if they have not done so in their role. Using this approach, creating what appear to be positive 'false memories' helps these people feel more confident to perform difficult elements of their role effectively.

Tips on How To Make Things Memorable

We now know a bit more about how the memory systems (sensory, STM, LTM) work in the brain. We also now know a little more about making memories last, through encoding (depth of processing, elaboration and distinctiveness). There are other effective ways to make things memorable. Below are a few other ways that will be helpful in considering memory a little deeper to enable learning in yourself and others.

Mnemonic techniques

Mnemonic techniques have been developed over the centuries to help people remember information. The ancient Greek orators would remember the content of their speeches by imagining a temple, with each argument of their speech pinned to a different pillar. When they spoke, they imagined moving through this mental space, encountering each argument as they went.

Novelty

Like we saw with distinctiveness earlier, novelty tends to stick in the memory. You may have commuted to work every day for years, but the only journey you remember with any detail is the one where someone fainted on the train, or the bus broke down, or something else out of the ordinary happened. Our brain, and in particular our hippocampus, is particularly attuned to novelty. Why? Because something unexpected tends to grab our attention, which we now know is the gateway to memory. This has been shown in animals and humans. A rat with a damaged hippocampus won't notice when you move something around in its cage, while the other rats will. A human presented with something unexpected – for example, a sentence like "The man spread butter on his shoe" – will show a distinctive pattern of electrical brain activity. In short, if you want it to be remembered, throw in a curve ball.

This is particularly useful to consider if you are working with a group or team to improve skills or create change – what novel approaches or exercises can you use that are different to traditional approaches?

Association

Staying with the hippocampus, associating items in memory is one of the hippocampus' main jobs – binding all the elements of a memory is crucial to allowing us to remember all the aspects of an event. People with damage to the hippocampus have particular trouble associating new names with new faces, supporting this view. This leads to a useful memory tip – when presenting something new, try to associate it with something that people are already familiar with. This could be in the form of an analogy, or through repetition. A great example, we can all recognise is how some brands have now made their product synonymous with particular days of the week (e.g. Crunchie: 'that Friday feeling') or the year (Pancake Tuesday = 'Jif Lemon Day'). If you are attempting to learn some new information or create a new habit, can you associate the rehearsing of the information or the doing of the action to something you already do habitually? For example, brushing your teeth, placing your shoes on your feet, or calling a loved one.

Feelings

The amygdala has a particular role in how we feel. For this reason, highly charged or 'emotional' events seem to have a 'privileged access' to memory, due to the amygdala's direct anatomical input to hippocampus. Therefore, strong feelings can leave a very lasting memory – sometimes positive (wedding days, celebrations) and sometimes negative (PTSD, trauma). Whether the feeling is positive or negative, imbuing content with an emotional valence will significantly increase its chances of being remembered.

Music

Similarly, music is a powerful memory trigger – partially because of the feelings often connected to particular musical pieces. Advertisers have long recognised the power of music in making products memorable, but research has also shown that dementia patients, even in later stages of the disease, can retrieve old memories when music is played for them.

Familiarity

When it comes to testing memory, recognition ("Did you see this?") is easier than free recall ("What did you see?"). Again, drawing on examples from advertising, attaching messages to familiar things – faces, settings, situations – seems to ensure memories will be retained. Celebrity endorsements are one application of this, where products become associated with a famous movie, music or sports star. Other campaigns centre around familiar environments or settings – the family dinner table, the sitting room sofa, the car. In tandem with the idea of association, familiarity can be a powerful tool in maximising memorability. Consider how the values that are most important and familiar to you can help you recall information or engage you with the doing of the new habit.

Unfinished

Referring back to the ideas of depth of processing and elaboration, one way to ensure deep encoding of material is to force the brain to do some work on that material. Thankfully, the brain needs very little encouragement to do this – it likes nothing better than to solve a problem or complete a pattern. In fact, it does this all the time without our noticing, filling in the hole in our visual world created by our blind spot. So, to engage the brain and make it process information at a deeper level, you should give it something to do – ask it to complete a pattern or fill in the blanks – for example, solve a problem related to the learning material at hand.

Learning and Long-Term Memory

New learning will not get stored in the LTM unless you get a chance to use it soon after learning. Plainly and simply, we forget most of what we have learned unless it is useful in the here and now! Make a decision on WHEN you are going to get started on the new behaviour and specifically WHERE. Many approaches to soft skills development are missing an approach that enables learners to elaborate on what they learn in the classroom.

When it comes to learning and habit change, it is clear that we forget the new way of doing something, because for example we haven't given the time to visualising what we want and visualising the outcomes. Therefore the information is not committed to LTM and we need lots of reminders –without which we forget and revert to our old ways.

Learning must be 'applied' rather than focusing on, for example, theory. It is imperative that we create more meaningful and elaborated opportunities to practice while in the learning room, to embed the learning in LTM.

Engaging Other People's Memory

How can you engage other people's memories more actively? Enrolling employees for a learning event has greatest value if they can apply their learning immediately; either actively in the learning session, or subsequently 'on the job'.

70:20:10 is an approach to organisational learning which can, if used effectively, capitalise on how memory works. It is often used to define the ideal balance for how to provide corporate learning and staff development opportunities. It proposes that on average, 70% of training should take place while on the job, 20% should be conducted informally through mentoring programs and 10% should be conducted formally through training sessions.[62]

In line with the 70:20:10 rule, the opportunity to apply and practice learning in the context of work gives the best results. In his book *The Learning Challenge*, Nigel Paine[63] refers to "at the moment of need" and "just in time" learning, and quotes Nick Shackleton-Jones' approach to learning "for people who care". Here, people care deeply about learning something because they have been challenged and want to or need to solve a problem. Therefore, they are motivated to learn.

The alternative – pushing learning on somebody who doesn't yet feel a need for it – is more challenging for the teacher or manager and for the student. Of course, this brings us back to establishing the 'WHY?' – why is it worth me putting effort into learning this now? And in what way will it benefit me even though I might not initially have seen a benefit to learning this new way of operating and behaving?

It is important to proceed with caution if you are applying the 70:20:10 rule. Research shows that if line managers are not trained to coach their colleagues on the job, then the 70:20:10 approach can fail to achieve the objectives of all involved. A 'coaching mind-set'[64] is considered to be a necessary prerequisite, along with specific skills and capabilities that facilitate effective managerial coaching.[65] An empirical study of exemplary managers found that being in a 'coaching mindset' was about empowering, helping, developing, supporting, and removing obstacles as opposed to traditional managing, which was often about telling, judging, controlling, and directing.[66]

STEP 4: MEMORY: WHEN & WHERE?

Now that you have your WHAT, WHY and HOW, it's time to work on WHEN & WHERE to help your memory get on board with your learning and habit change. If your role involves managing and developing people, also consider how you are supporting them to build this into their learning:

1) WHEN specifically are you going to take action? Write down the date and time. Perhaps write down a few dates and times into the near future so that you have lots of opportunities scheduled to build in the repetition required:

2) WHERE are you going to do it?

3) Write down any ideas you have regarding what could work for you on all of the below:

(i) Association – What in your current daily actions can you associate the action you are taking? For example, doing the thing as part of a morning routine - doing it at the same time every day helps create cognitive ease and uses the power of association to create automaticity quickly and easily.

(ii) Feelings – For example, encouraging people to share their success and challenges with their learning journey can evoke feelings and help things stick. Could you use an accountability buddy to do this with?

(iii) Unfinished – Could you challenge yourself to do even five minutes of research, reading on the topic of the change you are trying to make, to fill in some blanks?

(iv) Mnemonic techniques – if you have learned a new piece of information, could you create a mnemonic for it? If you have created a new habit, could you create a mnemonic for the steps you have to take regarding for example, your specific habit loop (see more in Step 5)?

(v) Music – What music can inspire or get you positively focused? This can really help your 'HOW'.

*(vi) Personal values – What are your top three values in how you live your life? (See **Book 1** for an exercise to discover your personal values and how aligning to them can keep you moving forward once the initial motivation dissipates).*

(viii) Novelty – This is a tough one to create for actions that need to be repeated. But if you are creating a learning experience for your team or colleagues, is there a new way to approach it?

Note: If you prefer to print out a version of the worksheets with the questions for all steps, rather than write in this book, please see **www.adaptastraining.com/books**.

STEP 5: DEDICATION: HOW MANY?

Learning is what most adults will do for a living in the 21st century.

Alfred Edward Perlman

You've heard people say, "I'm too old to change", "I'm too old to learn anything new", or even "The damage has been done, it's too late for me".

In Book 1 of this series, **Our Learning Brain**, I discussed creating new neural pathways. In this book, Richard has explained that incoming data is held in STM (working memory) and will be quickly lost if not consolidated. How well we encode a memory is critical to how effectively we will be able to recall it at a future point. And this applies regardless of what age we are!

The storage of information takes place across several neurons and brain systems at the same time. So that the learning sticks, your neurons need to be allowed the chance to repetitively communicate with each other. Once or twice is not enough. Repetition is key for consolidation. So:

> **Firstly**, we will look at the importance of repetition to help you apply it to your own learning and habit change.
>
> **Secondly**, we will look at creating conscious awareness of repetition by understanding habit loops
>
> **Thirdly**, we'll build on habit loops to explore habit stacking.

The Importance of Repetition – Repeat, Repeat, Repeat!

HOW MANY times and how often might you need to repeat in order to embed the learning and habit change long-term?

You've heard "Neurons that fire together wire together". Your brain is changing and rewiring itself constantly throughout your life, whether you want it to or not. Whatever you do a lot, you get better at. If you practice listening a lot, you become a better listener. If you practice football, you become a footballer. If you sit on the couch every day, you get better at sitting on the couch. You don't have to think about doing it, you just do it. When two neurons fire at the same time repeatedly, chemical changes occur in both so that the two tend to connect more strongly. This is one of the reasons why just doing something once doesn't create a habit or change. You have to repeat and practice. The more the neural pathway is used, the more on alert it is and quick to fire. Neural pathways become more myelinated with use. The myelin sheath is fat and it's like the plastic coating on your wires. It makes the signal go more quickly. Myelin is more active in childhood and adolescence, and can be less active in adults, but it's still working for us as adults. If something is wired, we can disrupt or re-route the wiring to create new habits and learn new things. We need to then practice the actions that reinforce those thoughts, behaviours and actions until they become automatic.

Various Functional Magnetic Resonance Imaging (fMRI) studies show the important role of the areas of the brain associated with the neurotransmitter, dopamine, in the learning process. Remember, dopamine is the brain's chemical reward, often increasing just in anticipation of that reward.

When we eat in response to hunger, feel the warmth of the sun, or receive a smile for an action taken, the brain releases a short dopamine burst to signal its pleasure and give us a quick reward.

This dopamine reward mechanism also serves to reinforce the neural connections in the associated network, strengthening it with each repetition of the thought or behaviour that caused it. This facilitates, amongst other chemicals of learning discussed in **Part 1** of this book, the biological process that embeds learning.[68]

Initial neuron changes after learning something new are only temporary. In order for them to be retained long-term, we have to repeat, repeat, repeat.

Ultimately, it comes back to how badly you want something. As with the first steps, 'WHAT' and 'WHY': do you habitually imagine WHAT you want your outcome to be and then repeat the steps to get there?

Stronger and faster connections between neurons form through repetition. The challenge for us is to actually make time for repeating. Daily duties, tasks and immediate needs tend to be prioritised in life. But structuring in deliberate opportunities for repetition after new learning will increase the return on investment.

The study of memory and repetition by psychologists dates back to experimental psychologist Hermann Ebbinghaus (1850 to 1909).[69] His most famous finding, the 'forgetting curve', describes the exponential loss of information that one has learned.

The sharpest decline in forgetting occurs in the first 20 minutes, though the decay is significant through the first hour and the curve levels off after about one day. Ebbinghaus discovered that people forget what they've learned at a predictable rate. Thousands of studies have since replicated this finding.

He used nonsense syllables (like "WID, ZOF") as his stimuli, ensuring they would be free of confounding associations in his own memory, and learned a long list of them to 100% accuracy, then tested himself again at regular intervals, plotting the gradual loss of information from his memory, which reached an asymptote (a line or curve that approaches a given curve arbitrarily closely) at about 20%. He then explored the effects of re-learning the list at different times, showing that each instance of re-learning increased the asymptote by an additional 20%, so with three re-learning sessions, recall plateaued at around 80%.

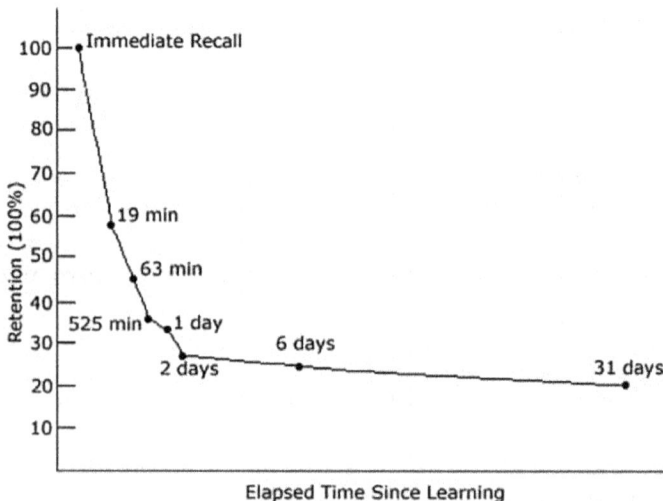

Figure 5: Ebbinghaus' Forgetting Curve.

Subsequent studies looked at the effect of how these re-learning sessions were spaced out, comparing massed (many sessions in a short time) with spaced (the same number of sessions over a longer period) learning. It has been reliably shown that massed learning is good for recall over the short term, but for longer-lasting retention of information, spaced learning is better.

This explains why cramming before a test might get you through that particular exam, but you will probably not remember the information a few weeks later. This was also nicely demonstrated recently in a clever study which compared binge-watching of TV shows with more traditional one-episode-per-week exposure. Those who binge-watched had significantly poorer recall of the plot of the shows compared to the spaced exposure group.[70]

Learning and then engaging in new behaviour in short bursts, spaced over time, and with constructive feedback, is much more effective for long-term integration than trying to do too much too quickly.

If you read **Our Learning Brain**, you will recall what I said about how long it takes to break an old habit or learn a new skill so that it is embedded long-term. Philippa Lally and colleagues from the Cancer Research UK Health Behaviour Research Centre based at UCL Epidemiology and Public Health looked at how long it took people to reach a limit of self-reported automaticity for performing an initially new behaviour (that is, performing an action automatically).[71] They found that it takes on average 66 days (not 21!) to change a habit, with people often taking beyond 230 days of repetition to change habits long-term.

Conscious Awareness of Habits: Habits Loops

How are we going to remember to repeat our actions so that we can embed the learning and habit change? Two concepts that are useful to consider in bringing more conscious awareness to repetition – both the old repetition we want to interrupt and the new repetition we want to create – are habit loops and habit stacking.

To understand a **habit loop**, we need to break things down into a routine (the behaviour you want to change), a cue (that causes or starts the behaviour) and a reward (the benefit / gain and avoidance of loss you get from that behaviour). The reward is often the motivator, as is the avoidance of loss of something.

Basically, we are motivated to perform a current habit because it provides us with a reward. We've talked about dopamine and the reward centres of the brain. Our brain is often rewarding us for things that aren't necessarily good for us. Its drive is to feel good and safe!

MIT researchers, Catherine Thorn and her colleagues discovered the **habit loop** while experimenting with rats running mazes. They discovered that during initial maze runs the rats' brains generated a great deal of activity in the cerebral cortex. However, navigating the mazes after numerous repetitions required less activity in the cerebral cortex, even in the parts of the brain governing memory. The brain converts the sequence of actions, 'chunking' them to the primitive basal ganglia, reserving the cerebral cortex for higher or more intensive functions. The main component of the basal ganglia is the striatum. For example, this area of your brain is active when you're driving the same route home from the supermarket that you've been taking for months or years, driving all the turns, stopping when you need to stop and arriving home without any conscious memory of having actively paid attention to what you were doing!

The cue for a habit can be anything that triggers the habit. Cues most generally fall under the following categories: a location, a time of day, other people, an emotional state, an item, a sensation, or an immediately preceding action.

An example for me of one of my not so healthy habits, my love of chips from the fish and chip shop. The cue here is the smell (sensory experience) of the vinegar wafting from a fish and chip shop (location).

An example of one of my healthy habits is juicing vegetables and ginger every morning. The positive cue for me here is when I walk into my kitchen first thing in the morning, the juicer is the largest contraption on the kitchen countertop (item and location) and is difficult to ignore. I never put it out of sight in a cupboard. Otherwise it will be too easy to forget about it. The juicer's role is to cue me to make the juice, as well as to actually drink the juice!

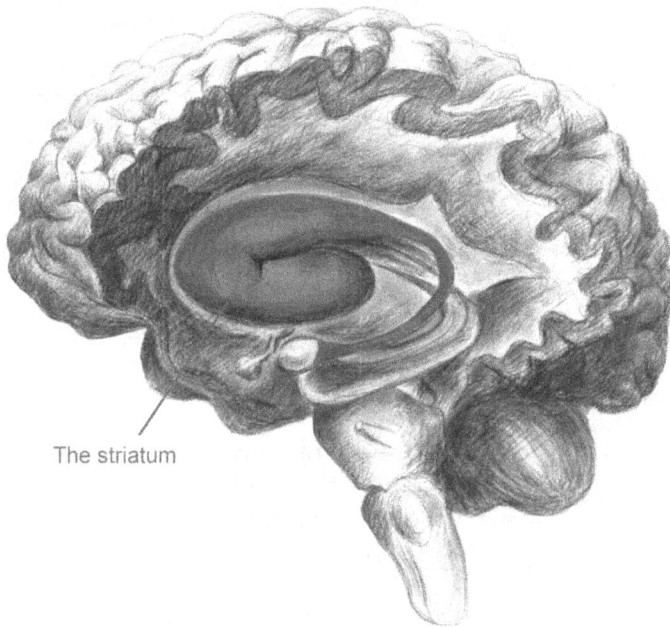

Figure 6: The Striatum.

The cue tells the brain to go into automatic processing mode and into the routine; in the first case for me it is: "Go on, you've been working hard all day, have a bag of chips". In the second instance, "It's time to start a new day, it's going to be a busy one, let's start by getting some healthy vegetables juiced and into you quickly". If the cue is there, it takes effort to resist the routine. The routine is the behaviour you want to perform less of, or more of.

The reward is the reason the brain decides the previous steps are worth remembering for the future. The reward provides positive reinforcement for the desired behaviour, making it more likely that you will produce that behaviour again in the future. The reward can be anything, the tangible taste of vinegar, salt and soft potato on my tongue and the full feeling in my stomach after the chips, to the intangible feeling of satisfaction that I have started my day in a healthy way once I have had my juice.

Get to know your cues, through experimentation and identify the rewards that come from your habitual routines. This is important because these habit loops can get in the way of learning and habit change even when we are motivated to change. They are stored in your striatum, and it can take a great deal of effort to override them!

For example, another manager we worked with, Kate, had an extremely busy role, managing a team of 10 people. Kate had some challenges with delegation. For example, one of the individuals on her team, Jessica, was tasked with getting a document to Kate weekly which summarised information that needed to be sent to an important internal client. Kate received an email from Jessica every Friday morning with the document attached. Regardless of what Kate was doing at the time, she always dropped what she was doing and got focused on fixing small mistakes on the document that Jessica had sent. Jessica always made small mistakes, which because of the size of the document amounted to 30-45 minutes of Kate's Friday mornings spent making corrections.

The routine here was that Kate fixed mistakes made by Jessica. The cue was the document received by email around the same time every Friday morning. The reward for Kate was knowing that she would come across as a professional to her client (if all spellings were correct and all sentences were structured correctly). The problem with this behaviour or routine, was that Kate rarely got to break for lunch or finish her working day on time on a Friday because this task ate into her day. This habit was a problem! But of course, she had all her stories and limiting beliefs to back it up: "I'm the only one who can get these documents completed perfectly, I've been doing it for years"; "I'm a perfectionist, which is necessary for my role. Other people don't work at the standard I expect"; "If I don't personally get this done, my client will lose faith in me for other projects"; and "People are not forgiving of mistakes".

Kate needed to learn to trust Jessica (and as it turned out, she needed to learn to trust some of the other people on her team also) to fulfil this task completely to the level that she and their clients expected. If Kate kept correcting Jessica's documents, Jessica would never learn to fix these mistakes and Kate would need to keep spending time she did not really have available to her, checking and double checking the documents. Kate therefore needed to change the cue. As the cue was the email that she received from Jessica every Friday morning, she finally started (not without putting up many arguments to me) to give Jessica permission to send the document directly to their client. Our hope was that if Jessica knew the document would go directly to the client, she would be more likely to double and triple check the document before she sent it on. If the client came back with questions because spellings were incorrect then this was a learning opportunity for Jessica. By changing this cue, Jessica and Kate eventually changed the routine. In a very short period of time, having committed to this relatively low-risk change in behaviour, Kate began to trust and delegate much more effectively and realised her team were capable of more than she had given them credit for. Because Kate empowered Jessica to take control of this outcome, Jessica indeed performed as was needed.

Conscious Awareness of Habits: Habit Stacking

Now considering the habit loop concept, can you think of something that is a really well engrained habit – something you do every day without fail? Maybe it's brushing your teeth every day or making a cup of coffee. It could even be going to the closet to take your clothes out for the day ahead. Now consider, what is the new habit you wish to create? Is it to do some exercise every day, or eat an apple every morning, or say "I love you" to your partner every day? Habit stacking, (popularised by author S.J. Scott in his book **H**abit Stacking: 97 Small Life Changes That Take Five Minutes or Less)[72] requires you to pair the new habit you wish to create with an old existing habit. Your habit stack could be: "After I switch the coffee maker on to heat up, I grab an apple and eat it immediately". Or "Before I open the closet to take my clothes for the day ahead, I tell my partner 'I love you'". Or "When I put my toothbrush back in the holder every morning after brushing my teeth, I run on the spot for 30 seconds". This is habit stacking. Habit stacking is a type of implementation intention: a very simple plan of 'If...Then' or 'If X, then I will Y' or 'before X, I will Y' or 'after X, I will Y'

You consciously specify that you will eat an apple when you have switched the coffee maker on. The 'X' is what we refer to as the critical situation, in this case switching the coffee maker on. The 'Y' is a goal-directed response, the thing you want to do more of, for example, eating an apple every day. Over time you pair the 'X' and the 'Y', and the 'Y' eventually becomes as automatic as the 'X'. Remember at the outset of this book, I mentioned that it takes conscious effort to make the unconscious become conscious, so that we can work with it. If you can pay attention to what you are doing automatically (i.e. turning the coffee-maker on), you can pair it consciously with the apple eating. Over time, both actions become unconscious, and you have now created the new habit you wished to create (the eating of the apple!).

Where else might habit stacking help you? As mentioned above, Kate had a constant struggle with delegation. She decided to give habit stacking a go to see if this could help her delegate more effectively. She started with something very simple: a daily task list she drew up every morning. She had been creating a daily task list since she was at university and therefore it was a very well engrained habit. This task list became her 'X'. The 'Y' needed to be something that would enable her to delegate some tasks from this list. She decided that every morning as she sat down at her desk and before she picked up a pen to draw up her list (X), she had to 'pair' this 'X' with sending one email to a colleague (any one of the 10 people on her team) to set up a 10-minute call for 12.30pm on that same day (her new 'Y').

Then while writing her task list, she would have to find at least one item to discuss with that colleague at 12.30pm that she would delegate to that individual. She therefore paired sitting down at her desk to start writing her daily task list (the critical situation 'X', which was inevitable for Kate) with sending an email to her colleague to set up a quick call at 12.30pm (the goal-directed response 'Y'): *"If I sit down at my desk to write my daily task list, then I will send an email to one of my colleagues to set up a 12.30pm 10-minute meeting."*

Now that we have considered the importance of and the various ingredients of repetition, it's time for you to consider how you will build in repetition or 'HOW MANY' to your WHAT, WHY, HOW, WHEN & WHERE.

STEP 5: DEDICATION: HOW MANY?

1) What can you do to guarantee repetition to create this change or embed your new learning?

2) When learning new skills or creating new habits in the past, what worked to help you create repetition?

3) What is / are your current cues with the behaviour you want to change?

4) What is / are the current rewards you get from that behaviour?

5) What new cues can you adopt to create your new behaviour?

6) What new rewards can you get from your new behaviour?

7) Can you create a habit stack? For example, If X, then I will Y".

8) What will be happening for you to know you have repeated enough times and for long enough (weeks / months)?

Note: If you prefer to print out a version of the worksheets with the questions for all steps, rather than write in this book, please see **www.adaptastraining.com/books**.

STEP 6: ENVIRONMENT: WHO?

Environment trumps will. WHO can be your ally in making change? For many of us, the people we are surrounded by and WHO we spend our time with has a huge impact on how we behave and HOW we learn.

There are items we need to seriously consider in the WHO:

>**Firstly**, WHO is in our environment?
>
>**Secondly**, WHO are you receiving feedback from?
>
>**Thirdly**, if you are a manager, what role are you taking in embedding change? You are part of the WHO in encouraging your people to learn and grow.

WHO is in our Environment?

As discussed in **Part I**, the brain makes shortcuts and can only process so much information at once. We are more reliant on environmental triggers than we'd like to think. We are our environment. WHO we surround ourselves with has a big impact on how we operate.

If you are looking to learn and make changes, it is extremely challenging to keep positively focused if we are surrounded by people WHO moan about their lives, WHO gossip and WHO are not open to learning new things. If you are working in such an environment, consider how this is serving you in being the person you wish to be. Perhaps there is another team you can request a move to, which enables you to develop new skills as well as be in a more positive frame of mind. If you have family and friends WHO operate this way, and harsh as it may sound, I'd highly recommend finding some new friends WHO have common interests to you, and spend a little less time with the others. If you work closely with a manager WHO is transactional, it will be very difficult for you to operate any differently. Therefore, WHO else can you spend time with? For example, a mentor WHO is more like the person, manager and leader you are looking to become?

WHO are we Receiving Feedback From?

Constant monitoring of progress by oneself, one's peers and one's superiors is tantamount to long-lasting change.

We know from Dr. Richard Roche that, by creating meaningful and elaborated opportunities to practice, long-term learning is more likely to occur. Meaningful connections create more permanent memories.

Whether it takes 18, 21, 66 or 265 days to create change, we all know it is difficult to commit to practicing to embed the change!

For this reason, it helps if we receive feedback from other people to know whether our attempts are working! Positive feedback or the anticipation of it during the learning process, increases dopamine,[73] thus consolidating the neural networks.

We all like to be told we are doing a good job! Feedback on performance and acknowledgment from others encourages us to repeat.

Feedback on Performance and Acknowledgment = Repetition

So many of us need to be reminded that it is working, even when we 'fall off the wagon'. We must track behaviours ourselves, and / or get feedback on how that behaviour is being noticed by others and how it is impacting others.

Progress is about recognising what needs to change, doing it repetitively and getting feedback, especially with a focus on how improvement is being noticed by others.

It is important, therefore, to work with people over a period of time regarding accountability and feedback. WHO can be your learning buddy or habit change accountability partner?

Your Role as a Manager in Embedding Change

If you are a people manager, part of your role is to keep noticing the attempts of your staff to try things a new way, and to continuously support them as they learn. This encourages repetition and therefore consolidation.

Many line managers require reminders from the learning & development professional (in-house or external) and the learner themselves on the part they have to play in the learning process of each of the individuals on their team. It is everybody's responsibility to ensure the learning sticks. And therefore it can be useful to set up some kind of accountability partner, or a buddy pairing where people are reminded of, and encouraged towards, what they said they would do, learn or change.

If you are managing other people, have you assisted them in imagining what they desire the outcome to be? How it will benefit them? How will life and work be different? People will only repeat new behaviours if they can clearly see the personal gain or benefit and / or that they will lose out on an opportunity if they don't apply what they are learning.

In my experience, everything I have shared with you in this book can be used to support your people and teams with change.

If you are managing someone who is attempting to make change, it may require you to write reminders to check in with your colleagues on the change they are trying to make regularly. You might still be checking in with them on that change they want to make in six months' time, but accountability and repetitiveness lead to new habits forming eventually.

I know as well as you do that it's challenging to fit all of our responsibilities in every day and every week. However, if you help people feel good when attempting to make changes, they are much more likely to succeed. People must see results and one of the roles of a manager is to support and coach.

Add to that, learning is no longer just the responsibility of the learning and development, talent management or HR team. Managers are becoming increasingly held responsible for developing their employees and facilitating their learning.[74] In fact, if you are currently or planning to be a manager of people, pay attention: research shows that YOUR ongoing feedback to your colleagues about their progress with the changes that both you and they are making is one of the most important ingredients in successful learning and habit change.[75]

In many organisations, people have performance appraisal conversations with their manager, getting clear on objectives and changes that might need to be made. However, as yet, in many organisations (not all) many managers do not perceive their own role as being responsible for supporting the learning process. Many managers see learning as a 'distraction' rather than a necessity! And many line managers are not being taught how to support learning and the habit change required to learn new ways of operating.

There has recently, been a big move towards training managers to coach. This is a very worthwhile move as employees move away from acceptance of the manager as being responsible for telling, controlling or administering and having a task-focused orientation.

Hunt & Weintraub (2002)[76] identified the main characteristics of effective managerial coaches as:

> An attitude of helpfulness.
>
> Less need for control.
>
> Empathy in dealing with others.
>
> Openness to personal learning and receiving feedback.
>
> High standards.
>
> A desire to help others to develop.
>
> A belief that most people do want to learn.

However, with this focus on training of managers as coaches, again my observation is that these managers are not being taught some fundamentals of how long-term learning occurs. They are generally not holding themselves or others accountable to embed the learning. If you've read through this book and are completing the worksheets (printable version of the worksheets at **www.adaptastraining.com/books**), you can hopefully now manage others more effectively in their learning.

Now in line with your WHAT, WHY, HOW, WHEN & WHERE, HOW MANY, who is your WHO? And how can you help them to support you or hold you accountable to your change and growth? The more specific and tangible you can get in your WHAT, the easier for them it will be to give you the feedback and support you require.

STEP 6: ENVIRONMENT: WHO?

1) WHO can you involve in supporting you (or hold you accountable) with this change?

2) Why will you have this person / these people support you (or hold you accountable) with this change?

3) How specifically will you have this person / these people support you (or hold you accountable) with this change? (face-to-face conversation, text, email, etc)

4) How are you going to build in feedback to yourself?

5) WHO else is going to give you feedback on the changes and progress? (Maybe this person / people is / are the same or different to those supporting / joining in this change or holding you accountable)

Note: If you prefer to print out a version of the worksheets with the questions for all steps, rather than write in this book, please see **www.adaptastraining.com/books**.

STEP 7: OBSTACLES: WHICH?

I don't know about you, but I know when I attempt to do something differently, the obstacles just keep magically appearing. I know all about creating daily routines and habit. And I know all about how my brain and body will do whatever it can to stop me from doing things differently. However, the obstacles always appear. This is why I urge you to consider your 'WHICH'?

'WHICH' refers to the obstacles that are sure to appear. It is therefore imperative in this section that we:

> **Firstly**, get clear on WHICH elements of life (internal and external) are going to be obstacles to change.

> **Secondly**, understand the power of Mental Contrasting using these obstacles.

> **Thirdly**, actively create Implementation Intentions with these obstacles.

WHICH Obstacles?

There will be many obstacles on the path to you achieving your WHAT. There will be external obstacles such as role responsibilities, child and parental responsibilities and many more. There will also be internal obstacles such as the limiting beliefs you hold about yourself, and the assumptions you are making about yourself and the change you are looking to make. There will also be the obstacle of time, which I would place on the threshold between internal and external obstacles.

The good news is that, by getting clarity on and using the obstacles that we think will most impede us from getting what we want, in fact these obstacles can help us to realise our plans.

This really important part of the process of learning and habit change has been discovered, developed and researched recently by Gabriele Oettingen, Professor of Psychology at New York University and the University of Hamburg, and author of *Rethinking Positive Psychology*,[77] who examined what stops us from moving from 'thinking about' to 'doing' change.

When we feel confident in ourselves, our brains often assume a goal is easier to acquire than it actually is. But our subconscious is hyper-efficient, as it allocates only as much energy as is needed to accomplish its goals. Anything more would be a waste. If it thinks that your goal will be extra-easy to accomplish, it will allocate less energy; less than is needed to achieve the intended outcome. For example, I was 80% there with this series of MAXIMISING BRAIN POTENTIAL books many years ago. Every time I planned to sit down to bring them to completion, I constantly underestimated the time to re-write and edit. I thought a few weekends would do it, and so my brain and body allocated less energy to getting it done.

As mentioned previously, your unconscious speaks in sensory experiences, WHICH is why your thoughts of accomplishment fail to help it understand the process of actually getting there. This phenomenon, called de-energisation, has been experimentally observed and induced, and leads to reduced goal commitment and attainment (Oettingen *et al.*, 2009).[78]

WHICH Obstacles?: Mental Contrasting

To combat this problem, Mental Contrasting was developed. Here's how it works:

> **Write down, or think about, several positive aspects associated with completing your goal.** For example, if you're trying to lose weight, those positive aspects could be related to your WHY: looking good, living longer, spending less on healthcare, feeling livelier, being able to stay active, getting your spouse to stop nagging you, etc. I generally recommend to my clients that they consider their personal values and how this change will bring them closer to living true to their values. It really is about considering our 'Why?'. For example, what recently drove a client to start exercising again after 20 years of very little physical activity was noticing how his seven-year-old is growing up to be a very physical and strong child, and realising that, if he wants to be able to keep up with him, he'll need to get fit! And what drove another client to start focusing on having his employees understand inclusion and promotion of more women into management positions was watching his own wife work long hard days,

making several sacrifices in her personal life in one role for eight years and live with the frustration of never getting promoted to the level she was clearly capable of and deserved.

Focus on the most positive aspects. There could be one especially large benefit, or a few smaller ones. Then take a few moments to visualise those benefits. The longer and the more detail, the better. This is connected to your HOW.

Now here comes the magic step:

Write down or think about several obstacles in the way of completing your goal. For example, if you're trying to lose weight, those obstacles could be: being tempted by snacks, purchasing unhealthy food while shopping, eating too much at dinner, lack of motivation to exercise, etc. For me, getting this book to the final finish line over a number of weekends throughout recent months, I have had to visualise many obstacles that might be more fun or even more relaxing.

Focus on the largest obstacles. There could be one especially large obstacle, or a few smaller ones. Then take a few moments to visualise those obstacles. Again, the longer and the more detail, the better.

WHICH Obstacles? Implementation Intentions

Now that you are clear on your obstacles and have gone through the process of mental contrasting, the next step is to use implementation intentions for each obstacle. You may recall I mentioned implementation intentions (otherwise known as habit stacking) previously. As a reminder, an implementation intention is an 'if-then' plan: 'If X, then Y'.

In the case of our obstacles, implementation intentions are really powerful for dealing with them. For example:

"If this obstacle appears, then I will do this or that".

Remember Catherine? Some of her 'if-then' plans for her obstacles were:

101

"If I am putting off having a coaching conversation with a colleague, then I will immediately find a minimum of 10 minutes in my calendar to plan for that conversation".

"If a seemingly important email comes in, I will ask myself the question 'by saying yes to responding to this email immediately, what am I saying no to'?"

"If I feel uncomfortable asking one of my colleagues for feedback, I will ask for it immediately rather than putting it off".

By bringing the obstacles that we all know are there somewhere into our conscious experience, and then working through implementation intentions on these obstacles, we are more likely to make the change. I know it sounds simple. However, in many of the studies[79] in which mental contrasting and implementation intentions were tested, participants were instructed to use the technique just once – taking just a few minutes. Afterwards, changes in behaviour were observed for up to several weeks and sometimes months.

Just like with all the steps, it's important to keep returning to the WHICH?: obstacles, mental contrasting and implementation intentions. Why? Because new obstacles will just keep appearing. That's life!

Now that you have been working through this book and are clear on your WHAT, WHY, HOW, WHEN & WHERE, HOW MANY, WHO, it's time to consider your WHICH:

STEP 7: OBSTACLES: WHICH?

1) Write down or think about several obstacles in the way of completing your goal.

2) WHICH are the largest obstacles?

3) Visualise those obstacles. What do those obstacles look, sound and feel like?

4) What will you do to overcome each and every obstacle you are aware of? Work through the 'If ... Then' for all internal obstacles (beliefs or stories you tell yourself) and external obstacles (a friend calls, or you have one more episode of a TV series to watch).

Note: If you prefer to print out a version of the worksheets with the questions for all steps, rather than write in this book, please see **www.adaptastraining.com/books**.

KEY TAKE-AWAYS

Embedding new ways of doing things, requires building conscious awareness of your habits and then choosing what you want to be.

Overcoming old ways of doing things and embedding new behaviours, will often require examining our self-identity, and focusing on the 'I can'.

Engaging as much of the brain and body as we possibly can, will assist long-term change.

Understanding that learning and habit change is a process, where many behaviours must be repeated many times to create long-term change will get you to where you want to be quicker:

STEP 1: CLARITY: WHAT?

STEP 2: CURIOSITY: WHY?

STEP 3: FEELING AWARENESS: HOW?

STEP 4: MEMORY: WHEN & WHERE?

STEP 5: DEDICATION: HOW MANY?

STEP 6: ENVIRONMENT: WHO?

STEP 7: OBSTACLES: WHICH?

I hope you have found the information in this book useful. I highly recommend you actively try out the various tips and tools throughout the book to support your learning and habit change. This can be a skill or competency you are looking to build at work, or an old habit you are looking to change. If you have not already, I urge you to work through the script of questions at the end of each of the Seven Steps by applying them to something you are looking to do more of, less of or differently in your life. If you would prefer to print out a version of the worksheet questions for the steps, rather than write in this book, see **www.adaptastraining.com/books**. You can print and use these worksheet questions over and over again, as you progress with your learning or habit change, or as you embark on new learning or changes in habits in the future.

Through following these steps, I have experienced so many people making significant changes:

> A director of product operations overcoming his fear of presentations and developing into a world-class presenter.

> A senior director who was told she would never make it to the C-suite, to reaching this aspiration less than18 months later.

> A group of leaders struggling to create a culture of coaching from the 'top' whilst also managing economic pressures, eventually committing to making this a reality in their workplace, where their own teams are now self-managing – giving the leaders more thinking time to expand into new markets and products.

> A team of start-up team leads moving from 12-hour working days and continual 'fire-fighting' to a supportive group of leaders who rise to an endless challenge with grace and tranquillity, having improved their work-life balance.

Let me know how it goes for YOU.

THE AUTHORS

DR. CELINE MULLINS

Celine is a Psychologist, Coach and Learning Specialist.

She founded **www.adaptastraining.com** and has over 15 years' experience working with individuals, teams and groups across multinationals, SMEs, governmental and educational agencies, in Ireland and internationally.

Celine works with leaders, groups and teams who are deeply committed to growth, positive change and making sustainable breakthroughs.

Celine obtained her BA (Hons) in Psychology at University College Dublin and her PhD at Trinity College Dublin. She also has a Certificate in Training and Development, Diploma in Statistics, Diploma in Personal and Executive Coaching, and Certificate in Cognitive Behavioural Coaching. She is furthering her studies currently, including Neuroscientific Coaching and Transpersonal Leadership Coaching qualifications.

She teaches the Cognitive Behavioural Coaching Module and the Organisational Coaching Module of the MSc in Personal and Management Coaching, University College Cork.

Celine has also appeared on TV, radio and in national press, and is a regular guest on podcasts, contributing psychological input on a range of topics, or sharing her experience of working with people and teams in organisations.

DR. RICHARD ROCHE

Richard is Senior Lecturer at the Department of Psychology, Maynooth University, where he has been employed since 2005, following undergraduate, postgraduate and postdoctoral study at Trinity College, Dublin. His areas of interest are neuroscience /

neuropsychology, particularly memory, stroke, psychosis and synaesthesia. He has published 28 research articles, several book chapters and two books, *Pioneering Studies in Cognitive Neuroscience* and *Why Science Needs Art: From Historical to Modern-day Perspectives.*

He was Associate Editor for *Frontiers in Human Neuroscience* from 2013 to 2016. He has received over €1,225,000 in research funding, and is currently involved in collaborations between Maynooth University and the Stroke Unit of Tallaght Hospital in Dublin, as well as the National Rehabilitation Hospital, Dún Laoghaire. He served on the Neuroscience Ireland committee from 2005-2014, as Vice-President 2010-2012 and President 2012-2014, and was the founding President of the Irish Brain Council in 2013.

He is also strongly committed to science outreach and public engagement, and has given an Ignite talk at Science Gallery's Mindfields at Electric Picnic 2016, performed for BrightClub Dublin in 2017, as well as hosting '*The Brain Box*', a 2-part radio documentary about the brain on NewsTalk 106-108FM.

See more at: **http://publicationslist.org/richard.roche**.

NOTES

1   Aristotle (Philosopher). Quote available at:
     https://www.passiton.com/inspirational-quotes/7103-we-are-what-we-
     repeatedly-do-excellence-then (Accessed: 12 August 2020).

2   Sandberg. S. (2013). *Lean In: Women, Work, and the Will to Lead*.
     London: WH Allen.

3   Masie, Elliott (Educational expert). Quote available at:
     https://www.quotemaster.org/qc33d6da75aa8cfc681d709c5dcab11a6
     (Accessed: 12 August 2020).

4   Alabaster, P.G. (Chief Marketing & Communications Officer, Centric
     Brands). Quote available at: https://www.workflowmax.com/blog/50-
     inspirational-leadership-quotes-from-women (Accessed: 12 August
     2020).

5   Bersin, Josh (2018). 'New research shows "heavy learners" more
     confident, successful, and happy at work'. Available at:
     https://www.linkedin.com/pulse/want-happy-work-spend-time-
     learning-josh-bersin/?published=t (Accessed: 12 August 2020).

6   James, W. (1890). *The Principles of Psychology*. Henry Holt & Company.

7   Goleman, D. (1984). 'New view of mind gives unconscious an expanded
     role'. *The New York Times*. Cites Donchin, E., Director, Laboratory for
     Cognitive Psychophysiology, University of Illinois. Available at:
     https://www.nytimes.com/1984/02/07/science/new-view-of-mind-gives-
     unconscious-an-expanded-role.html (Accessed: 12 August 2020).

8   Wood, W. *et al.* (2002). 'Habits in everyday life: thought, emotion, and
     action'. *National Library of Medicine*. PMID: 12500811. Dec 2002;
     83(6):1281-97.

9   Moscoso del Prado, Fermín (2009). 'The thermodynamics of human
     reaction times' Available at: https://arxiv.org/abs/0908.3170 (Accessed: 12
     August 2020).

10   Kaku, Michio (Theoretical physicist). Quote available at:
     https://www.brainyquote.com/quotes/michio_kaku_615181 (Accessed: 12
     August 2020).

11   Galla, B. & Duckworth, A. (2015). 'More than resisting temptation: Beneficial
     habits mediate the relationship between self-control and positive life
     outcomes'. *NCBI*. PMCID: PMC4731333. Sep 2015. 109(3): 508-525.

12   Stanovich, K.E. & West, R.F. (2000). 'Individual differences in reasoning:
     Implications for the rationality debate?'. *Behavioural and Brain
     Sciences*, 23: 645-726.

13   Kahneman, D. (2011). *Thinking Fast and Slow*. New York: Farrar, Straus &
     Giroux.

14   Azevedo *et al.* (2009). 'The human brain as a linearly scaled-up primate
     brain'. *J. Comp. Neurol.* Available at:

http://www.suzanaherculanohouzel.com/azevedo-et-al-2009-j-comp-neur/ (Accessed: 12 August 2020).

15   Hasselmo, M.E. (2006). 'The role of acetylcholine in learning and memory'. *NCBI*: PMCID: PMC2659740.

16   Columbia University, Author Unknown(2018). 'Receptor related to neurotransmitter serotonin to boost memory formation'. *Medical Press* (May 10), pp. 1-2.

17   Kraus, C. *et al.* (2017). 'Serotonin and neuroplasticity: Links between molecular, functional and structural pathophysiology in depression'. *National Library of Medicine.* PMID: 28342763. Epub: Mar 22.

18   Rose, S.R. & Orlowski, J. (1983). 'Review of research on endorphins and learning'. *National Library of Medicine.* PMID: 6348097.

19   Blum, K., Liu, Y., Shriner, R. & Gold, M.S. (2011). 'Reward circuitry dopaminergic activation regulates food and drug craving behavior'. *Current Pharmaceutical Design*, 17(12): 1158-1167.

20   Volkow, N.D., Fowler J.S. & Wang, G.J. (2002). Role of dopamine in drug reinforcement and addiction in humans: Results from imaging studies'. *Behavioural Pharmacology*, Sep 13(5-6): 355-366.

21   Rácz, I. (2013). 'Neuroplastic changes in addiction'. *Frontiers in Molecular Neuroscience*, 6: 56.

22   Schultz, W. (1998). 'Predictive reward signal of dopamine neurons'. *Journal of Neurophysiology*, 80: 1–27.

23   Sapolsky, Robert M. (2005). *Monkeyluv: And Other Essays on Our Lives as Animals*. New York: Scribner / Simon & Schuster.

24   Kahneman, D. & Tversky, A. (1979). 'Prospect theory: An analysis of decision under risk'. *Econometrica*, 47(4): 263-291.

25   Boyatzis, R. (2011). 'Neuroscience and leadership: The promise of insights'. *Ivey Business Journal.* Nov. 26, pp. 1-4.

26   Morin, Amy (2015). 'You're only as good as your worst habits'. *Forbes.* February 24.

27   Cai *et al.* (2014). 'Brain plasticity and motor practice in cognitive aging'. *Frontiers in Aging Neuroscience*, 6: 31.

28   Maxwell, John C. (2011). Quote available at: https://www.azquotes.com/quote/878534 (Accessed: 12 August 2020).

29   Einstein, Albert (Physicist). Quote available at: https://www.oreilly.com/library/view/john-adairs-100/9780857081759/cmp74.xhtml (Accessed: 12 August 2020).

30   Frank, C. *et al.* (2014). 'Mental representation and mental practice: Experimental investigation on the functional links between motor memory and motor imagery'. *NCBI.* PMCID: PMC3990621.

31   Frank, C. *et al.* (2016). 'Perceptual-cognitive changes during motor learning: The influence of mental and physical practice on mental representation, gaze behavior, and performance of a complex action'. *National Library of Medicine.* PMCID: PMC4705276.

32   Pascual-Leone, A. *et al.* (1995). 'Modulation of muscle responses evoked by transcranial magnetic stimulation during the acquisition of new fine motor skills'. *Journal of Neurophysiology*, 74(3).

109

33   Morin, L. & Latham, G. (2001). 'The effect of mental practice and goal setting as a transfer of training intervention on supervisors' self-efficacy and communication skills: An exploratory study'. *Applied Psychology*, 25 December.

34   Bartlett, F.C. (1932). *Remembering: A Study in Experimental and Social Psychology*. Cambridge: Cambridge University Press.

35   Unknown. Quote available at: https://www.habitsforwellbeing.com/20-quotes-to-inspire-self-care/ Quote #4. (Accessed: 12 August 2020).

36   Hansen, Mark Victor. Quote available at: https://www.goodreads.com/quotes/100005-don-t-wait-until-everything-is-just-right-it-will-never (Accessed: 12 August 2020).

37   Dove, R. (2019). 'The Knowledge: Gwyneth Paltrow on how to create a lean body shape'. *Telegraph*, 29 July.

38   Miller, William (1983). 'Motivational Interviewing with problem drinkers'. *Behavioural Psychology*, 983(11): 147-172.

39   Martins, Renata K. & McNeil, Daniel W. (2009). 'Review of motivational interviewing in promoting health behaviors'. *National Library of Medicine*. PMID: 19328605. Jun, 29(4): 283-93.

40   Fredrickson, B.L. (2009). *Positivity*. New York: Three Rivers Press.

41   Gaffney, M. (2011). *Flourishing*. Dublin: Penguin Ireland.

42   Rampton, J. Quote available at: https://quotesdot.com/quote/make-no-mistake-about-it-bad-habits-are-called/101961 (Accessed: 12 August 2020).

43   Emerson, Ralph Waldo. Quote available at: https://www.goodreads.com/quotes/14132-cultivate-the-habit-of-being-grateful-for-every-good-thing (Accessed: 12 August 2020).

44   Wood, A.M., Froh, J.J. & Geraghty, A.W.A.. (2010). 'Gratitude and well-being: A review and theoretical integration'. *Clinical Psychology Review*, November, 30(7): 890-905.

45   Stillman, J. (2016). 'Gratitude physically changes your brain', citing Achor, S., author of *The Happiness Advantage* (2010) and founder of the Institute of Positive Research and GoodThinkInc. Article available at: https://www.inc.com/jessica-stillman/the-amazing-way-gratitude-rewires-your-brain-for-happiness.html (Accessed: 12 August 2020).

46   Gaffney, M. (2011). *Flourishing*. Dublin: Penguin Ireland.

47   Seligman *et al.* (2005). 'Reflecting on positive events and identifying signature strengths increased happiness and reduced depressive symptoms among website visitors for six months'. Available at: https://www.wiseinterventions.org/posters/reflecting-on-positive-events-and-identifying-signature-strengths-increased-happiness-and-reduced-depressive-symptoms-among-website-visitors-for-six-months.

48   Seligman, M.E.P. (2002). *Authentic Happiness: Using the New Positive Psychology to Realize Your Potential for Lasting Fulfilment*. New York: Free Press.

49   Robbins, A. Quote available at: https://www.goodreads.com/quotes/157336-when-you-are-grateful-fear-disappears-and-abundance-appears (Accessed: 12 August 2020).

50   Edmondson *et al.* (2016). 'Understanding psychological safety in health care and education organizations: A comparative perspective'. *Research in Human Development*, 13(1): Role of Psychological Safety in Human Development.

51   Project Aristotle. 'What makes a team effective at Google?' Available at: https://rework.withgoogle.com/guides/understanding-team-effectiveness/steps/introduction/ (Accessed: 12 August 2020).

52   Wanless *et al.* (2013). Setting-level influences on implementation of the responsive classroom approach'. *National Library of Medicine*. PMID: 23065349. Feb, 14(1): 40-51.

53   Gostick, A.R. & Christopher, S. (2008). *The Levity Effect: Why It Pays to Lighten Up*. New York: John Wiley & Sons Inc.

54   Billington, D. (2001). *Life is an Attitude: How to Grow Forever Better*. Washington: Lowell Leigh Books.

55   Knowles, M. (1990). *The Adult Learner: A Neglected Species*. Houston: Gulf Publishing Co.

56   Lewis, M.B. & Bowler, P.J. (2009). Botulinum toxin cosmetic therapy correlates with a more positive mood'. *Journal of Cosmetic Dermatology*, 8: 24-26.

57   Lewis, D. (2005). Cited in: 'One smile can make you feel a million dollars'. *The Scotsman*. 4 March.

58   Carlson, N.R., Martin, G.N. & Buskist, W. (2004). *Psychology* (2nd edition). Harlow: Pearson Education.

59   Atkinson, R.C. & Shiffrin, R.M. (1968). 'Human memory: A proposed system and Its control processes'. In Spence, K.W. & Spence, J.T., *Psychology of Learning and Motivation* (Volume 2, pp. 89-195). New York: Academic Press.

60   Blake *et al.* (2015). Available at: https://www.sciencedaily.com/releases/2015/03/150327101157.htm (Accessed: 12 August 2020).

61   Craik, F.I.M. & Tulving, E. (1975). 'Depth of processing and the retention of words in episodic memory'. *Journal of Experimental Psychology: General*, 104: 268-294.

62   The 70-20-10 Model for Learning and Development. (1980s). Available at: https://trainingindustry.com/wiki/content-development/the-702010-model-for-learning-and-development/ (Accessed: 12 August 2020).

63   Paine, N. (2014). *The Learning Challenge*. London: Kogan Page.

64   Hunt, J. & Weintraub, J. (2002). 'How coaching can enhance your brand as a manager'. *Journal of Organizational Excellence*, 20 February.

65   Ladyshewsky, R. (2010). 'The manager as coach as a driver of organizational development'. *Emerald Insight*, ISSN: 0143-7739.

66   Ellinger, A.D. & Bostrom, R.P. (2002). 'An examination of managers' beliefs about their roles as facilitators of learning'. *Management Learning*, 33(2): 147-79.

67   Perlman, A.E. Quote available at: https://www.quotes.net/quote/16342 (Accessed: 12 August 2020).

68 Grill-Spector, K., Henson. R. & Martin, A. (2006). 'Repetition and the brain: Neural models of stimulus-specific effects'. *Trends in Cognitive Science*, 10(1): 14-23.

69 Ebbinghaus, H. (1850-1909). *The Forgetting Curve*. Available at: https://www.csustan.edu/sites/default/files/groups/Writing%20Program/forgetting_curve.pdf (Accessed: 12 August 2020).

70 Horvath, J.C. *et al.* (2017). 'The impact of binge watching on memory and perceived comprehension'. Available at: https://firstmonday.org/ojs/index.php/fm/article/view/7729/6532 (Accessed: 12 August 2020).

71 Lally, Philippa *et al.* (2009). 'How long does it take to form a habit?' Available at: https://www.ucl.ac.uk/news/2009/aug/how-long-does-it-take-form-habit (Accessed: 12 August 2020).

72 Scott, S.J. (2014). *Habit Stacking: 97 Small Life Changes That Take Five Minutes or Less*. New Jersey: Oldtown Publishing LLC.

73 Wittmann, B.C., Schott, B.H., Guderian, S., Frey, J.U., Heinze, H-J. & Düzel, E. (2005). 'Reward-related fMRI activation of dopaminergic midbrain is associated with enhanced hippocampus-dependent long-term memory formation'. *Neuron*, 45(3): 459-467.

74 Ellinger *et al.* (2006). 'The manager as coach: A review of empirical literature and the development of a tentative model of managerial coaching', p.1. Available at: https://www.ufhrd.co.uk/wordpress/wp-content/uploads/2008/06/18-1_ellinger_beattie_hamlin_wang_trolan.pdf (Accessed: 12 August 2020).

75 Gentry, B. & Young, S. (2017). 'Busting myths about feedback: What leaders should know'. *Center for Creative Leadership*. White Paper.

76 Hunt, J. & Weintraub, J. (2002). 'How coaching can enhance your brand as a manager'. *Journal of Organizational Excellence*, 20 February.

77 Oettingen, G. (2015). *Rethinking Positive Thinking: Inside the New Science of Motivation*. New York: Penguin Random House LLC.

78 Oettingen, G. *et al.* (2009). 'Motivation', Chapter 8. Available at: https://acmelab.yale.edu/sites/default/files/2010_motivation.pdf (Accessed: 12 August 2020).

79 Cross, A. & Sheffield, D. (2019). 'Mental contrasting for health behaviour change: A systematic review and meta-analysis of effects and moderator variables'. *Health Psychology Review*, 13(2).

ADAPTAS

Adaptas consists of a team of experts with a range of backgrounds, combined to impact personal and organisational change. Working with individuals, groups and teams in organisations internationally, we have a strong focus on narrowing the gap between learning and the real world, and on linking development with outcomes in a way that is effective and lasting. This approach brings people on a truly unique and engaging experience of learning, enabling them to be more effective and impactful in their roles.

Popular topics include:

Leadership Development: Leading Self and Leading Others Authentically.

Creating and Maintaining High Performing Teams.

Resilience, Stress Management and Mental Toughness.

Brain Management: Cultivate the brain's potential for productivity, creativity and peace.

Maximising Brain Potential to Manage Change and Learn.

Developing Emotional Intelligence.

Communication: Influencing, Difficult & Coaching Conversations & Presentations.

Negotiation – Understanding your Thinking and Behaviour to avoid a 'one style fits all approach'.

Creating and Maintaining a Happier and More Accountable Culture: Values & Behaviours.

Improvisation in Business for an Ever-Changing World.

Adaptas has been an early adopter of new technologies that bring an added layer of immersion to learning in organisations, including Virtual Reality and Augmented Reality learning sol

www.ingramcontent.com/pod-product-compliance
Lightning Source LLC
Chambersburg PA
CBHW072128090426

42739CB00012B/3109